DREAM CARS

Sam Philip

Contents

DREAM CARS

What makes a dream car? Put another way, why do some four-wheeled lumps of metal and plastic and rubber send otherwise rational humans into paroxysms of automotive rapture, while others stir no more emotion than a particularly forgettable chest freezer or microwave?

It's more than mere fastness, though that always helps. Massive horsepower and fighter-jet-crushing acceleration rarely hurt a car's bid for fantasy status, but they don't tell the whole story. Some dream cars are less than face-alteringly fast. Some are downright slow. We're looking at you, Morgan 3 Wheeler. After all, if desirability was directly correlated to top speed, we'd all lust after A380 Airbuses. Most of us don't.

Bleeding-edge technology? Maybe, maybe not. No question we're suckers for cars employing NASA-grade know-how to warp physics, but many of the most reverie-inducing machines of the twenty-first century haven't packed a whole lot in the way of technology. Or, in some cases, any technology at all. We're looking at you, Morgan 3 Wheeler.

Maybe, then, it's about fitness for purpose: cars that do exactly what they say on the tin, with no extraneous fluff nor compromise. Cars with a single aim – be it flattening the Nurburgring lap record or plodding indestructibly to the North Pole – instead of trying to be all things to all drivers. Then again, who could fail to be seduced by an all-rounder like the Audi RS6, a car that can play sensible family estate but secretes supercar-smashing pace?

Hmm. Perhaps a dream car is one that's more than the sum of its parts, one that somehow turns a jumble of oily, metally components into something … organic. Alive. Or maybe that's just the sort of soppy anthropomorphism that causes ladies of a certain age to dress up their Pomeranian in a waistcoat, and sagely state that Mr Tibbles is very sensitive to people mentioning his weight.

Truth is, dream cars exist beyond scientific deduction or mathematical explanation. But one thing's for sure. Far from witnessing the predicted decline of fizz-generating automobiles, the twenty-first century has seen more addictive, petrolhead-piquing cars than any era before: dream cars of every flavour, from warp-speed hyper-hybrids to impossibly lissom lightweights, from tyre-immolating super-saloons to indestructible off-roaders. This sturdy tome contains 100 of the very best.

If you love cars – and if you don't, what are you doing here? – there's never been a better time to be alive. Dream on.

GREAT BRITAIN

Call us mad, bulldog-saluting jingoists – and many do – but can any other nation on earth boast a more magnificently diverse array of cars than Her Majesty's Glorious Island of Blighty? From Caterham's skeletal lightweights to the opulence of Rolls-Royce, from the straight-outta-the-thirties chaps at Morgan to the knee-trembling, timeless designs of Aston, Britain does it all. And does it with that quintessential blend of fine engineering, stiff upper lip and industrial quantities of tea that once built an empire. True, the UK's global influence may have faded a little since the glory days of the mid-1800s, but when it comes to cars, Britannia still rules the waves.

ASTON MARTIN

DBS

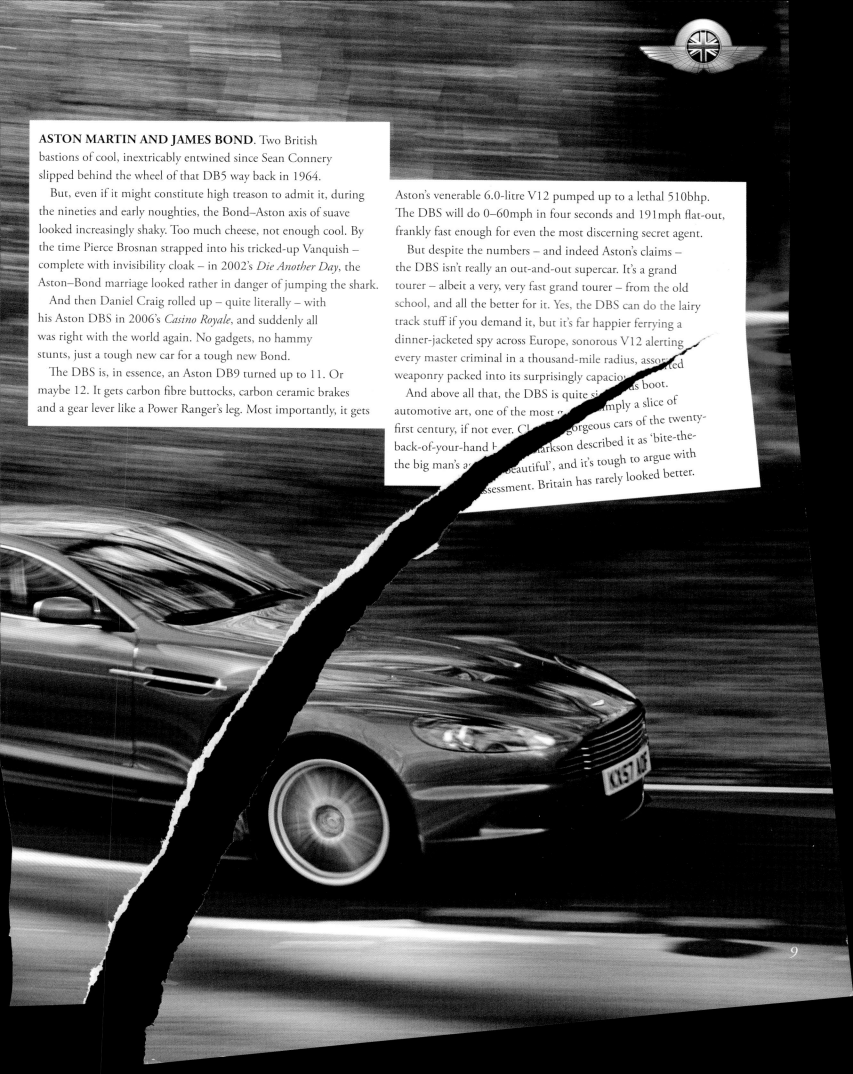

ASTON MARTIN AND JAMES BOND. Two British bastions of cool, inextricably entwined since Sean Connery slipped behind the wheel of that DB5 way back in 1964.

But, even if it might constitute high treason to admit it, during the nineties and early noughties, the Bond–Aston axis of suave looked increasingly shaky. Too much cheese, not enough cool. By the time Pierce Brosnan strapped into his tricked-up Vanquish – complete with invisibility cloak – in 2002's *Die Another Day*, the Aston–Bond marriage looked rather in danger of jumping the shark.

And then Daniel Craig rolled up – quite literally – with his Aston DBS in 2006's *Casino Royale*, and suddenly all was right with the world again. No gadgets, no hammy stunts, just a tough new car for a tough new Bond.

The DBS is, in essence, an Aston DB9 turned up to 11. Or maybe 12. It gets carbon fibre buttocks, carbon ceramic brakes and a gear lever like a Power Ranger's leg. Most importantly, it gets

Aston's venerable 6.0-litre V12 pumped up to a lethal 510bhp. The DBS will do 0–60mph in four seconds and 191mph flat-out, frankly fast enough for even the most discerning secret agent.

But despite the numbers – and indeed Aston's claims – the DBS isn't really an out-and-out supercar. It's a grand tourer – albeit a very, very fast grand tourer – from the old school, and all the better for it. Yes, the DBS can do the lairy track stuff if you demand it, but it's far happier ferrying a dinner-jacketed spy across Europe, sonorous V12 alerting every master criminal in a thousand-mile radius, assorted weaponry packed into its surprisingly capacious boot.

And above all that, the DBS is quite simply a slice of automotive art, one of the most gorgeous cars of the twenty-first century, if not ever. Clarkson described it as 'bite-the-back-of-your-hand beautiful', and it's tough to argue with the big man's assessment. Britain has rarely looked better.

ASCARI
A10

**IT'S FAIR TO SAY THE ASCARI A10'S PARENTAGE
WAS A TRIFLE CONFUSED.** It was named for an
racing driver and conceived by a Dutch billionaire
Klaus. Its engine came from a BMW M5. But th
British as Marmite and polite queuing. Not c
was built on an industrial estate in Banbury
a machine that required a seriously stiff u

  This was a scary brute. The A10 ma
be a friendly, modern supercar, one
and makes the driver feel good ab
Oh no. The A10 was driving at
as luxurious as an army Land
brakes nor traction control
was as manly as Lawrenc

  'The only thing kee
realized Jeremy as h

ROLLS-ROYCE

PHANTOM

DROPHEAD COUPÉ

'THE DROPHEAD DOESN'T FOLLOW THE HERD,' said Captain Slow when he reviewed the convertible Phantom back in 2007. 'It has its own idea of what a luxury car should be.'

As Mr May has long bemoaned, for most modern manufacturers 'expensive' has become synonymous with 'sporty': the finest, priciest cars getting huge wheels, rock-hard suspension and an obsession with going round the Nurburgring faster than Sabine Schmitz. But that's not how Rolls, erm, rolls.

Because though the Phantom Drophead Coupé is very, very expensive – £300,000 of expensive, to be precise – it isn't the least bit sporty. In the world of Rolls-Royce, in fact, you rather suspect 'sporty' is a dirty word.

Instead, the 2.6-tonne Drophead concentrates on being, in a word, exquisite. So luxuriously appointed is this convertible that it makes even the poshest Germans and Italians look a trifle … plain. Its fabric roof is lined with cashmere. You can have it in any one of 44,000 shades of paint. Rather than carbon fibre or race-grade aluminium, the rear deck is fashioned from teak, the same posh wood finish you'd find on a luxury yacht. When you take your Phantom Drophead Coupé in for servicing, a man from Rolls will give the wooden decking a thorough oiling, as you would a cricket bat.

Chopping the roof off something as vast as a Phantom is no minor operation. To stop the Drophead Coupé from folding itself in half at the sight of a corner, the Rolls-Royce Posh Welding Department – this may not be its official title – added an extra 460 feet of welding to the Phantom chassis. Even so, this isn't a car for flinging round bends, never mind the Nurburgring. This is a car for elegantly floating along a Mediterranean boulevard, venerable 6.75-litre V12 humming discreetly in the background. Athletic as Buckingham Palace the Drophead Coupé may be, but it's perhaps the coolest car in the world.

CAPARO T1

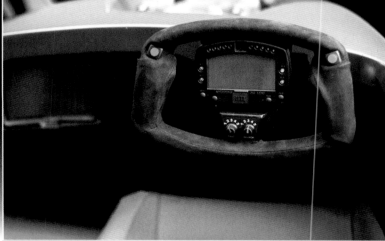

IN RECENT YEARS, IT HAS BECOME FASHIONABLE FOR START-UP MANUFACTURERS – particularly British start-up manufacturers, for some reason – to announce their latest arrival as 'an F1 car for the road'. But no manufacturer has ever interpreted the brief quite so literally as Caparo with its T1.

Designed by the team behind the original McLaren F1, this is as extreme as a machine can be without having to surrender its tax disc. A flyweight two-seater, with the passenger staggered behind the driver, the T1 packs a 3.5-litre race engine developing 575bhp. In a car that weighs about the same as a patio heater, that means a 0–100mph time of just five seconds. From standstill to triple figures in the time it takes George W. Bush to read this sentence.

'You can forget Enzos. You can forget Koenigseggs,' screamed Jeremy from under his helmet when he tested the T1 in 2007. 'This is in a different league. This is acceleration like I have never experienced …'

There are, as Clarkson discovered, a few tiny problems with the T1. Firstly, it seems to break quite often, sometimes in novel and fiery ways. Secondly, it costs way over £200,000, and will therefore only be bought by Premiership footballers. Thirdly, and perhaps most importantly, the T1 is not very nice to drive. That's 'not very nice' in the sense of 'utterly terrifying'. Understeer, oversteer, lack of grip – the Caparo has the lot. 'If you try to go round a normal roundabout at a normal speed in this, you're going to have a huge accident,' warned JC.

Even so, on the track rather than the open road, the T1 remains a devastating weapon. Stig recorded a lap of just 1m10.6s, the fastest a road-legal car has ever made it round the *Top Gear* test track. However, the Caparo couldn't keep its place atop the leaderboard: with its low, race-car nose, it's incapable of clearing a speedbump and therefore ineligible for the Power Laps board. Caparo wasn't lying: this truly is an F1 car for the road. Just not a bumpy road.

MINI
COOPER

BMW'S ATTEMPT TO REVIVE THE MINI COULD HAVE BEEN A BRANDING CAR CRASH, a retro mish-mash as shameless and unfaithful to the original as, say, the new VW Beetle.

But the new Mini is far from a car crash, and not just because BMW remembered to stay at least reasonably true to the original's brief. Whatever you think of the styling, and the fact that it's not especially, well, mini any more, there's no denying this is one of the best-engineered, finest-driving little cars on the planet.

This is a car built for the human behind the steering wheel, and to hell with everyone else. You sit low, with your legs straight ahead, behind a shallow windscreen. Just like in a Porsche 911. Even with the basest engine, this is a specialist coupé, not a mass-market hatch.

The real clue to how fanatically the Mini is engineered lies in that rear axle. Where most small cars make do with cheap-and-cheerful torsion beam rear suspension, the Mini is treated to a posh multilink set-up, usually the preserve of posh saloons and proper sports cars. This has the unhappy effect of rendering the Mini's boot even smaller, but makes it simply sublime to drive.

OK, BMW didn't entirely resist the temptation to go retro-twee. The Mini's huge central speedometer is not only naff but entirely useless, easier to see from the car behind than from the driver's seat. ('What's that, officer? How fast was I going? Well, I … oh, you could actually see my speedo?') And if it's your only family car, you'd better hope your family aren't planning on developing legs.

Perhaps in response to the demands of parents who own children with legs, BMW has got carried away with its Mini success in recent years. From the wilfully eccentric Clubman to the bloated Countryman, the firm's attempts to expand the brand haven't quite hit the mark. The simple, straightforward, two-door Mini Cooper remains the sweetest car in the line-up, all 120-odd horsepower of it. Like the original, you have to work hard for every mile per hour, but the rewards are great.

R500

IN 1957, COLIN CHAPMAN DEVISED THE
LOTUS 7, a lightweight, low-cost sports car that, even
by the standards of the day, was hardly cutting edge. In 1973,
Caterham Cars acquired the rights to the 7 design … and spent the
subsequent 40 years trying to figure out just how fast it's possible to
make a bolt-it-together-yourself kit car from the 1950s go.

Pretty damn fast, as it turns out. The R500 shares its basic
underpinnings with every 7 that has gone before, but represents
Caterham's fastidious devotion to shaving every last unnecessary
gram from the car. The rear-light houses are rendered in
aluminium, while the body panels are bespoke and even thinner
than those of the standard 7. The boot cover is made of something
called 'carbon leather', presumably harvested from the hide of
carbon cows. All of which adds up to a 9kg weight saving. That
might not sound much, but when you consider the entire R500
weighs barely half a tonne, even with driver and petrol on board,
these tiny margins matter. It also means that, with a 2.0 litre
Duratec four-cylinder pumping out 263bhp, the R500 can boast a
power-to-weight ratio of over 500bhp per tonne.

What all that maths equates to, in the
real world, is this: a 0–60mph time of 2.88
seconds, the sort of acceleration usually reserved for
particles in the Large Hadron Collider. It also equates to a
car that requires every iota of your concentration to drive fast.
In fact, to drive at all. With your bottom parked right on its rear
axle, you can feel every shimmy and slip of the R500's rear tyres.
And they slip a lot. But as Stig proved, in the hands of a creature
with superhuman driver talent, the R500 is searingly fast. The
white-suited one wrestled the Caterham round the *Top Gear* track
in a time of just 1m17.9s, one of the very fastest laps ever and
quicker than machines with triple its power. Top work, Colin.

ASTON MARTIN

V12 VANTAGE

THE FORMULA WAS A SIMPLE ONE: Aston's biggest engine – a bellowing 6.0-litre naturally aspirated V12 – in its smallest car, the Vantage. (OK, technically the Cygnet is Aston's smallest car, but that's (a) just a rebadged Toyota iQ and (b) one of the most vile cars to defile our roads this century, so we can safely ignore it.) The outcome was one of the most spectacular British sports cars in history – so spectacular, in fact, that it reduced the rarely mute Clarkson to near-silence when he tested it in Scotland.

'It is fantastic. It is wonderful, wonderful, wonderful,' nodded the big man in a moment of uncharacteristic reflection. 'What it makes me feel, though, is sad. I just can't help thinking that cars like this will soon be consigned to the history books. I have a dreadful feeling that what I'm driving here is an ending …'

Thankfully JC – for once – was wrong. The V12 Vantage wasn't an ending, but just the beginning, spawning a roadster, a faster still 'S' version and even a super-limited Zagato edition, gloriously rebodied by the legendary Italian design house.

You can tell the V12 from the less ballistic Vantages by the great carbon fibre snouts in its bonnet, the fatter sills and splitters, and the look of mild terror on the face of the driver attempting to keep it pointing the right way. The V12 Vantage is a wild, palm-sweating ride, a throwback to the days when sports cars were hairy and not for the faint-hearted.

This is a car with no interest in going slowly, restless at low speeds, impatient to get moving. But wind it out and you'll discover a deliciously meaty confection. True, on a twisty track the V12 Vantage wouldn't see which way a Porsche 911 GT3 or Ferrari 458 went, but this isn't a car about split-second lap times or purple sectors. It's a brawny British brute, and all the better for it.

LAND ROVER
DEFENDER

IN 1948, THE VERY FIRST LAND ROVER ROLLED OFF THE PRODUCTION LINE. It was called, inventively, the Land Rover. Pitched as Britain's utilitarian alternative to America's Willys Jeep, the boxy, simple Land Rover quickly gained a reputation for being virtually indestructible. Its go-anywhere abilities and millennial lifespan made it an instant hit with farmers, aid missions and local militias.

You know what they say: if it ain't broke, don't fix it. And Land Rover, clearly deciding its original concept wasn't so much unbroken as unbreakable, continued to produce the no-frills 4x4, with only minor updates, for the next six decades or so. Admittedly it has undergone a few name changes, and a few concessions to modern safety and emissions regulations, but today's Defender can trace its lineage directly to the very first Land Rover: indeed, a handful of the modern Defender's parts are said to be interchangeable with those of the 1948 original.

Which means, unsurprisingly, that the Defender is not the last word in twenty-first-century sophistication or cutting-edge technology. This is as back-to-basics as machines come,

trading cruise control, remote-control tailgates and 3D sat nav for bulletproof mechanicals that can be fixed with a hammer if you become stranded atop an Alp. On the road, the Defender is borderline unbearable, crunching and clanking and wheezing its way through the gears with all the vim and vigour of an elderly donkey. Reaching 30mph is an achievement; 70mph is a distant dream.

But lead the Defender away from tarmac and onto nastier terrain, and instantly this wheezing donkey comes into its own. Swamp, waist-deep mud, river, glacier: the Defender will clamber over it all with gentle grace and impossible tenacity.

But now, after more than 60 years in production, the Defender looks set to die, kyboshed by ever-more stringent emissions regulations, not to mention a buying public who desire at least a modicum of comfort from their off-roaders.

Even if production ends, there'll still be plenty of Defenders on the road. A few years ago, Land Rover estimated that 70 per cent of all the Defenders (and its predecessors) ever built were still running. Likely they still will be at the dawn of the twenty-second century.

NOBLE

M600

THE NOBLE M600 IS BUILT IN A SHED OUTSIDE OF LEICESTER. It is powered by a hopped-up version of the 4.4-litre V8 engine from a Volvo XC90. As formulas for creating the perfect supercar go, this one doesn't sound very promising.

But from such humble roots has come one of the most enervating supercars of recent times, a mid-engined, rear-drive brawler that makes even a Lamborghini Aventador or McLaren 12C seem tame in comparison. This may have something to do with the two giant turbos that Noble has bolted to that humble Volvo block.

On the M600's dash lurks an aluminium twist-switch with the option of Road, Track or Race. 'Road' gives you 450bhp, which is frankly plenty in a car weighing less than 1200kg. 'Track' ups the power to 550bhp, while 'Race' delivers a deranged 650bhp, which arrives in a terrifying, turbocharged burst between 4500rpm and the 6900rpm redline, accompanied by a hard-edged V8 cry and a manic flutter from the wastegates when you lift off the throttle.

In 'Race' mode, the M600 is fearsomely rapid. The Noble gets to 60mph from rest in three seconds, to 120mph in 8.9 seconds, and then on to 225mph. Acceleration from 40 to 60mph takes one second; from 100 to 120mph takes two seconds.

There's no clever double-clutch auto box here, rather an old-school six-speed manual and an old-school clutch pedal. Don't expect much in the way of electronic help, either. Yes, you get traction control – the button covered by a genuine flip-up cover from a Tornado fighter jet – but the Noble eschews antilock brakes and electronic stability control as a bit weedy. Why? If race cars don't need them, so neither does the M600.

All of which means it should be a fearsome monster to drive hard, even on a track. But it isn't. So magical is the M600's chassis, so accurate its steering, that it telegraphs every change of grip in high definition. This is, unquestionably, one of the very best cars ever to emerge from a Leicestershire shed. High praise indeed.

C-X75

IN 2010, JAGUAR REVEALED ITS GORGEOUS C-X75, a hybrid hypercar to rival the McLaren P1, LaFerrari and Porsche 918.

It was built to achieve four aims, individually simple but wildly contradictory. Hypercar looks. Veyron performance, which meant 0–62mph in three seconds flat and triple figures three seconds later, along with a 220mph top speed. The ability to do 40 miles or so in all-electric mode. And the combined carbon-dioxide output of a Toyota Prius. No, really.

Trying to jam these four aims into one low, wide car caused, unsurprisingly, a bit of a headache. So Jaguar called on its friends at the Williams F1 outfit for a bit of help with the electronic side of things.

What Jaguar and Williams came up with was so radical it made the 918, P1 and LaFerrari look almost straightforward. The C-X75 would use a 1.6-litre four-cylinder engine with a turbo and supercharger, revving to a dizzying 10,200rpm and developing –

wait for it – 500bhp. But that wasn't all. On top of that, the C-X75 packed a pair of electric motors, one for each axle, developing almost 200bhp each. Which makes the C-X75 a 900bhp, four-wheel-drive hybrid.

It meant the superJag could run in silent, electric-only mode … but who wants to do that when you've got 900bhp to play with? Flat-out, the hyperJag would easily have kept pace with its McLaren, Porsche and Ferrari rivals. Perhaps it might even have gone quicker.

Sadly we'll never know. Jaguar's original aim was to build 250 cars, at a cost of some £750,000 each. But in 2011, in the depths of the global financial crisis – and despite having done the hard stuff by making all the technology actually work – Jaguar nixed the C-X75 project. Though some of its technology will find its way onto road cars – in admittedly less spectacular form – this stunning hypercar shall never reach series production. The C-X75 will remain one of British motoring's great 'what ifs' …

ARIEL

ATOM
500

'THE NORMAL RULES ARE,' MUSED JAMES WHEN HE TESTED THE ATOM 500, 'that if you have a big heavy car and you want it to go fast, you have to put a big powerful engine in it. If you have a small light car and you want it to go fast, you don't need to put such a big engine in it. So what happens if you take a very light car and put a very big engine in it?'

The Atom 500, that's what happens. It takes a special sort of madness to look at the 'standard' 275bhp Atom and think, 'You know what this car really needs? A whole load more power.' After all, the standard Ariel Atom was fast enough to reconfigure Jeremy's face, fast enough to turn James May into a human spaniel. But the chaps at Ariel didn't get to where they are today – a nice barn in Somerset, to be specific – by being rational and sensible about things. So to create the Atom 500, out went the old four-cylinder, and in came a

V8 created by bolting together a pair of Hayabusa superbike engines, all wrapped up in the same spindly scaffold frame as the lesser Atoms, albeit supplemented with a pair of huge wings front and rear. This meant a 500bhp output in a car weighing around half a tonne, which even *Top Gear* maths can determine equals a power-to-weight ratio around 1000bhp per tonne. That's roughly twice the potency of the Bugatti Veyron, and slightly more than a small nuclear warhead.

The result? Quite simply one of the fast road-legal cars in history, a telepathic machine that responds to your inputs almost before you've made them. Ariel quotes the Atom 500's 0–60mph time at around 2.5 seconds, which is faster than just about anything short of an F1 car. If you want luxury, comfort or even a windscreen, look elsewhere. If you want the most elemental thrills on the planet, Somerset's the place for you.

ASTON MARTIN
ONE-77

WHEN ASTON MARTIN ANNOUNCED IT WAS BUILDING A MILLION-POUND SUPERCAR, the world took a sharp intake of breath. When it further announced this million-pound supercar would be limited to a production run of 77, said breath was intaken yet further. And when Aston revealed the first sketches of the One-77, which appeared to show a DBS that'd spent rather too long in the gym, well, there wasn't a whole lot of breath left for sharp intaking. But the One-77 isn't a DBS with some posh bits bolted on. It's a showcase of what Aston engineers can do with a near-unlimited budget and no production-line constraints. An Aston that pushes the boundaries of what an Aston can be, that pokes at the very edges of technology and design.

The headline stats are impressive enough: a Cosworth-engineered 7.3-litre V12 developing 730bhp makes the One-77 the most powerful, naturally aspirated production car on the planet. Technically mid-engined, so far is the V12 nestled behind the front axle, the One-77 gets from nought to 62mph in about 3.5 seconds, with a top speed somewhere north of 220mph. But it's what lurks beneath those figures that really puts the One-77 in a league of its own. Constructed around a carbon fibre monocoque with hand-beaten aluminium panels, the One-77 borrows technology from Germany's DTM racers, the most advanced front-engined track cars on the planet. Even the motors for the windscreen wipers are the same as those used in fighter planes.

If you're ever lucky enough to drive one, you'll find the One-77 brilliant and frustrating in equal measure. The engine is hypnotic, the power delivery a long, liquid experience. As the bypass valves pop open in the stainless steel exhaust at around 4000rpm, the One-77's respectable V12 bellow becomes an all-out heart-piercing scream, a noise that makes your heart pump faster. Frustrating? Afraid so. The six-speed automated manual gearbox is rubbish, clunky and slow and several decades behind the best transmissions out there. Will those 77 millionaire – nay, billionaire – owners care? Not a jot.

MORGAN

WHEELER

THE MORGAN 3 WHEELER ISN'T, WHEN COMPARED TO ANYTHING BUILT SINCE THE 1930S, VERY FAST.
Or very good at going round corners. Try to make it negotiate a bend at even modest pace and its super-skinny front tyres immediately relinquish grip, sending you sliding across the road haphazardly. Drive the 3 Wheeler down one of those single-lane country roads in which Britain specializes – where the edges have been scrubbed clean by car tyres but the centre is a lethal mix of gravel, grass and cow dung – and the rear-drive Morgan becomes as wayward as a horse on sheet ice, slewing from side to side as its central rear wheel forlornly attempts to find grip.

It feels very, very old-fashioned. Mostly because … it is. This is a design that predates even Clarkson himself: a frame of steel tubing and wood, wrapped in aluminium panels behind a 2.0-litre V-twin engine nicked from a Harley-Davidson. And not much else. Radio? Cruise control? Any technology from the latter half of the twentieth century, let alone the twenty-first? Forget it.

Which makes the 3 Wheeler a rather puckering experience on the motorway. So low and open is the Morgan that, out on the highway, you live in terror of being ingested by an SUV or lorry. With no windscreen, pebbles become missiles, bugs become shrapnel.

Point is, the 3 Wheeler is – in lots of ways – rubbish. But it's also entirely brilliant. To drive the Morgan is to be instantly transformed into a WW1 fighter pilot on a kamikaze mission. The 3 Wheeler sounds like the sort of motorbike favoured by those suffering a mid-life crisis: a slow thud of two-cylinder, a glutinous growl that rises to a feral roar above 3000rpm. That's what the 3 Wheeler is really about: all the fun of a big ol' American chopper without the inconvenience of acquiring a bike licence, or of falling off and losing all your skin. The problem with most modern cars is that you have to be doing licence-losing velocities to get close to exploiting their potential. The Morgan provides a total sensory overload while never threatening legal speed limits.

RANGE ROVER
EVOQUE

A FASHION-LED SOFT-ROADER DESERVES NO PLACE ON A LIST OF THE COOLEST CARS OF THE TWENTY-FIRST CENTURY. SUVs, faux-by-fours, call them what you will: they're the scourge of today's roads, bought by feckless urbanites who imagine off-roading across the Sahara but in reality will never tackle terrain more challenging than the raked gravel track to Tilly's gymkhana. Soft-roaders are a compromise solution, a triumph of packaging over substance.

And the Evoque, on paper, should be the worst of the bunch. Designed with the aid of – and we're not making this up – Mrs Victoria Beckham, Posh Spice herself, it's even available in three-door form. An SUV for parents who love their kids enough to give them a nicer view of the road than they'd get from a Ford Focus, but not enough to give them their own doors? A triumph of marketing fluff over rational demand, surely.

Turns out, however, the Evoque is the ultimate do-anything superhatch. The fastest version – armed with a 240bhp four-cylinder turbo petrol engine – will, on a nasty British road, outpace even the finest hot hatches. Where Golfs, Astras and the rest get upset by broken tarmac, forcing the driver to ease off in the corners for fear of being bounced off the road by a cruelly placed pothole, the Evoque simply flows over even the worst surfaces: flat but never jarring, pliant but never sloppy.

But the Evoque isn't just at home on the road. Unlike most soft-roaders, which faint in the manner of a Victorian spinster aunt at the first sign of mud, sand or gravel, the Evoque is equally at home halfway up the side of a Scottish mountain or crawling across an Icelandic boulder-field. Or, as James discovered, tackling Nevada's rockiest canyons and sandiest sand dunes.

Most Evoque buyers, of course, are unlikely to re-enact Operation Desert Storm in their SUV, and will be content with off-roading no more extreme than mounting the kerb in their local supermarket car park. But what's wrong with having such a span of abilities in reserve? Call it future-proofing against global

CONTINENTAL GT

THE BENTLEY CONTINENTAL GETS A BAD RAP IN SOME PARTS. Firstly for being a 'footballer's car' – one beloved by the millionaire employees of the Premiership's richest clubs – but also for being a big, heavy brute, a prop forward beside the lithe Lotus Exiges and Caterham R500s of this world.

But to castigate the Conti for being less agile than a Lotus is to misunderstand its purpose, like complaining that Seb Vettel's Red Bull isn't much cop at towing a horsebox. The Conti isn't a lightweight sports-thing, but rather an unsurpassed grand tourer, a car to spirit you and your three beautiful companions from London to your Italian beachfront mansion without breaking sweat. And at crushing continents in one dismissive breath, the Continental is magnificent. The huge W12 engine – all six twin-turbocharged litres of it – serves up a great wave of power and a hypnotic soundtrack, a bassy wow-wow-wow that penetrates deep into your skull. This is a charismatic cruiser like no other.

And that's the Continental's finest trick. Despite Bentley being owned by the all-conquering Volkswagen Group, the GT doesn't feel like the product of the automotive world's mightiest empire. It doesn't feel … German. It feels very British and very, very expensive. The Conti boasts a cockpit packed with enough leather to give nervous cows recurrent nightmares for years to come: a bovine massacre, albeit a beautifully executed one. The burnished wood, the solid metal switchgear: it's all proof that Britain does luxury better than anyone in the world.

And yes, it's true that a disproportionately high number of Conti GTs are owned by the good burghers of Chelsea, Liverpool and Manchesters City and United, often in inadvisably lurid shades. But spec the Continental tastefully and it's an object lesson in class. Not to mention, as Mr May proved, a mighty effective mud-track rally car too …

IT'S A QUESTION WE'VE SURELY ALL ASKED OURSELVES AT ONE TIME OR ANOTHER. What do you buy if you (a) want something more exclusive than one of those oh-so-common Ferrari 458s or McLaren 12Cs, (b) have several million quid burning a hole in your very expensive trouser pockets and (c) suffer a mild obsession with old Citroëns, Audrey Hepburn and aubergines?

Well, you call McLaren's Special Operations division, who'll whip you up something just like the X-1. This strange, wonderful machine is, in essence, a McLaren 12C in drag. It retains that car's carbon chassis and 617bhp twin-turbo V8, but clothes them in the most extraordinary bodywork to appear on a road-legal car since Ettore Bugatti hung up his quill.

Why? Because that's what the customer – an anonymous though presumably not cash-poor McLaren regular – demanded. Said customer pitched up at McLaren's Special Ops unit brandishing an… interesting mood board, including,

apparently, a 1971 Citroën SM, the Guggenheim museums, an art deco clock, a grand piano, an eggplant and a black-and-white photo of Ms Hepburn. This is not a joke.

The result was very much a Marmite car: you either love the X-1, or hate it with a deep and violent passion. But whatever your feelings, you can't deny it's good to see a supercar that doesn't look like every other supercar out there. As Ferrari, McLaren, Noble and the rest cluster around the most efficient aerodynamic solution, the X-1 is proof there is another way. In many ways, it's a return to the golden days of the 1930s, where car designers were given total freedom to draw whatever they wanted, not just fiddle in the margins of a car created by engineers.

And hey, isn't it nice to know that, if your lottery numbers come up and you've always wanted a bespoke 12C – inspired by, say, the essence of pot pourri, Joan Rivers and a badger – that McLaren will make that dream come true?

LOTUS
EXIGE

THERE WERE GRAVE MUTTERINGS WHEN LOTUS ANNOUNCED ITS NEW EXIGE S. The old Exige was always Lotus's hardest, sharpest-edged track car, but, on paper at least, the new version sounded like it had gone a bit … soft.

It seemed to represent a heinous departure from Colin Chapman's too-often-repeated 'simplify and add lightness' motto. The old Exige's buzzy, 1.8-litre supercharged four-cylinder engine was to be replaced by a 345bhp V6 of almost double the capacity. The new car would be longer and broader, with wider tyres. It would have electric windows, stability control and – in a move as unexpected as finding a carbon fibre rear wing on a Land Rover Defender – even parking sensors. It would weigh 170kg more than the old Exige and cost, in top-spec trim, considerably more than a fully loaded Porsche Cayman. Very un-Lotus. Very worrying.

The grave mutterers shouldn't have worried. The Exige S is everything a Lotus should be … only more so. To drive the Exige S fast on a good road is perhaps to understand how Stirling Moss felt in one of those mad sixties F1 road races. There is much noise and speed, the steering wheel bucks around in your hands and it is terrifying yet somehow brilliant. It requires bravery, and rewards it.

Because the more you push the Exige S, the more assured it feels, the unassisted steering brimming with race-car feel, the front end changing direction with almost pathological determination. Bigger and heavier it may be, but this thing still packs the same power-to-weight ratio as a Porsche 911. It'll go from nought to 60mph in under four seconds and keep running to 170mph: that's supercar pace.

And supercar impractical. This is no long-distance GT: there's enough luggage space on board for your race helmet and nothing else at all. This is a car for track first and road second. A proper Lotus, then.

QT

WILDCAT

WAY BACK IN THE VERY EARLY DAYS OF *TOP GEAR*, ONE CAR CAUSED AN EMBARRASSING ON-AIR EJACULATION FROM RICHARD HAMMOND, an ejaculation he's been struggling to live down since.

The ejaculation ran something like this: 'I AM A DRIVING GOD!' And the car that caused it was the Bowler Wildcat, a just-about-road-legal Dakar buggy armed with a 5.0-litre V8. A fibreglass-bodied, race-spec 4x4 that could outpace an Aston DB9 on the road, and just about everything in the world off it. A Land Rover-based headcase with its own on-board water supply. A car Hammond described as the best off-roader in the world. So what's happened to the deity-creating Wildcat since?

Well, a few years back, off-road parts suppliers QT bought the rights to the Wildcat brand from Bowler off-road, and set about adding a little liveability to the world's ultimate off-roader.

These things are all relative. Despite the addition of a stereo and a few storage bins, the Wildcat is still pretty much the last car you'd choose for a motorway schlep from Devon to Dundee. It is bare bones, brutal and basic. On the road it slews around, growling furiously, looking like it has just escaped from somewhere with a lot of biohazard signs.

But get the Wildcat away from the tarmac and suddenly it makes sense. That fully adjustable suspension absorbs boulders that would rip straight through any conventional off-roader, the Wildcat managing improbable speeds over terrain even a mountain goat would reject as 'a bit on the dicey side'.

This is, in truth, an all-terrain supercar, one designed to withstand many thousands of miles of the harshest treatment known to carkind, pummelled by dunes and sand and fearsome temperatures on South America's Dakar rally. In truth, the Wildcat will survive absolutely anything you can throw at it, short of driving into the magma chamber of an active volcano while simultaneously using its cabin as an impromptu nuclear test facility.

The Wildcat will leave you battered and bruised, but feeling decidedly alive. Feeling, in fact, like a driving god.

MONO

THE TWENTY-FIRST CENTURY HAS WITNESSED COUNTLESS ATTEMPTS TO UPDATE THE CLASSIC BRITISH LIGHTWEIGHT. These attempts have generally been the work of men in sheds with lofty ambitions but limited mechanical aptitude. Almost without exception, these attempts have been rubbish.

And it'd be easy to pass off the single-seat Mono as another garage-build special, another 'race car for the road' from a British start-up company, with a supercar-crushing power-to-weight ratio and a chassis constructed from bits of old washing machine and blind hope. But the Mono – from Lancashire-based outfit Briggs Automotive Company – is different, and not just because of its antisocial seating plan. Though the headline stats are suitably devastating – 280bhp and a 540kg kerbweight means 519bhp per tonne, 0–60mph in 2.8 seconds and a top speed of 170mph – it's the Mono's sheer quality that sets it apart. This is a pocket-sized masterpiece of engineering.

'We wanted to make the ultimate formula racer for the road,' says BAC boss Neill Briggs. 'And the ultimate racers are single-seaters. In terms of dynamics, you always have a compromise with offset seating, so just one central seat was always part of our original concept. We wanted to take the classic British lightweight concept into the twenty-first century …'

In truth, the BAC looks like it overshot that runway by a century or two. Up close, this looks less British lightweight, more extraterrestrial visitor from the future.

The details are delicious. Directly behind the centre seat lurks a 2.3-litre, naturally aspirated Cosworth four-cylinder – originally a Ford Duratec unit, but treated to a dry sump, forged pistons and conrods – butted up against a Xylon-coated, six-speed sequential gearbox. This transmission, borrowed from an F3 race car, drives the rear wheels through a limited-slip differential. About the powertrain, the Mono's pushrod suspension clings gracefully to its tub like a spider's web. Oh, in what is hopefully a world first, the Mono boasts a cockpit lining that's impervious to urine and human faeces. 'A synthetic suede originally developed for use in nursing homes, a variant of Alcantara designed to wipe clean after even the … worst accidents,' explains Briggs. 'Since the Mono's upholstery had to be weatherproof, we figured it was a good material to use.'

Here's hoping you never need test those claims. It'd be easiest to compare the Mono's driving position to sitting in a bath, but, unless you're either very short or have a very long bath, you'll actually be more upright in the tub than you are here. It's not uncomfortable – in fact, it's rather cosy – but finding your knees at the same height as your shoulders is an odd revelation. It's surprisingly comfortable pottering out on the road, too. Far from turning its driver's lower vertebrae into sneezing powder, the Mono rides sublimely, that open-wheel, pushrod suspension providing enough travel to smooth out Britain's finest potholes.

But this car isn't about potholes and pottering. Drop a couple of gears, pin the throttle and the Mono fires into the distance like a lit firework. As shocking as the momentous, massless acceleration is how easy, how natural it is to drive the Mono fast. Lying on your back in the dead centre of the chassis, a wheel at each corner, engine behind your head and a never-ending slug of even, addictive power, it's an act of instinct to thread the Mono through corners, rear tyres chatting convivially with your bottom. At the limit there's a frisson of understeer, but for the most part the BAC is deliciously neutral. It's easy to explore its limits, to push harder and harder without fear it'll spit you off. Despite the Mono's compliance on the road, there's not an ounce of squish or lean on the track. If you're used to road cars – even supercars – the Mono requires a recalibration of your brain to deal with its physics-warping abilities: brake deeper, turn in later, get on the power earlier.

Sure, 100,000 big ones is a lot for a car that requires you to strap your significant other to the roll-hoop if you're planning a romantic weekend away, but given its cortex-melting performance and engineering, the Mono could almost be regarded as a bargain. Classic formula successfully updated.

RANGE
ROVER

IT MIGHT, ON THE FACE OF IT, LOOK LIKE A GO-ANYWHERE 4X4, BUT THE RANGE ROVER ISN'T REALLY AN OFF-ROADER TO RIVAL A TOYOTA LAND CRUISER. The Range Rover is, in truth, a top-of-the-class limousine, a Mercedes S-Class for the minted type who finds an S-Class a trifle … unimposing.

There are few better places on the planet to sit than in the back of a Range Rover, especially one equipped with the loftily named 'Executive Seating', which trades the RR's standard three-seat bench for a pair of grand, individual armchairs, each equipped with massage function: thrones from which to gaze down upon the paupers below in their tiny, common cars. The wood and leather are the best in the woody, leathery business, the effect entirely business class. So convincing is the Range Rover at playing high-riding limo that you could easily forget it's a top-tier off-roader, too, one that'll attack jungle and swamp like a woodlouse-addled Bear Grylls. There's a mighty array of electronic gubbinry on board to help the Rangey keep chomping across sand, mud or molten lava, but you never feel the technology doing its thing, simply the march of relentless progress no matter what obstacles you put in front of the RR.

There's yet more cleverness within the Range Rover's skin. Land Rover chucked a billion quid at the development of a new all-aluminium monocoque that shaves 200kg or so from the weight of the old car, which means this big old bus is surprisingly agile, should you feel the need to chuck it round some corners. You won't. The Range Rover is all about the waft, about isolating you from the nasty real world beneath you. Armed with a wallet of sufficient depth, you can have your Range Rover with a 500bhp V8 petrol engine. In truth the big diesel is plenty enough, with its limitless torque and possibility of more than 200 miles between refuels. Whatever the engine, the Range Rover stakes a strong claim to the title of Greatest Do Everything Car on the Planet.

McLAREN
12C SPIDER

WHEN MCLAREN LAUNCHED ITS 12C COUPÉ, THE COMPANY'S FIRST ROAD CAR SINCE THE GENRE-DEFINING THREE-SEAT F1 OF THE EARLY NINETIES, boss Ron Dennis proudly proclaimed: 'We can prove scientifically that ours is the best sports car in history.'

Bold words, but Ron was right. Scientifically, objectively, the 12C coupé was, and is, an astonishing technical achievement. Built around a future-tech carbon fibre tub and utilizing every last drop of McLaren's Formula One know-how, it was devastatingly, ridiculously fast, lapping the *Top Gear* test track in a blistering 1m16.2s, almost three seconds faster than its closest rival, Ferrari's 458 Italia.

But Ron's scientific boast was precisely the issue with the 12C coupé. Yes, its performance was astonishing, but the Mac felt strangely digital against the 458's gloriously analogue experience. That twin-turbo 3.8-litre V8 served up obscene power, but didn't sing with the same passion as the Ferrari's naturally aspirated engine. Though the 12C would hurl itself anywhere you pointed it, and get there faster than you could ever imagine, it did so in clinical fashion, without the fizz and fingertip feedback of that cursed 458. The McLaren was the science, the Ferrari the art.

Until, that was, McLaren lopped the roof off the 12C to create the 12C Spider. A simple operation, but one that instantly gave the McLaren a personality to complement its physics-bashing performance. With that carbon tub, the roofectomy results in no loss of rigidity, the Spider handling with all the precision of its hard-top cousin. But opening the 12C to the outside world added a whole lot more noise and drama and weather.

Some might complain that, with its marginally higher roofline and marginally heftier kerbweight, the Spider is a lumbering slowcoach alongside the coupé: after all, it'll top out at a tardy 204mph where the hard-top will run all the way to 207mph. We suspect most will be prepared to make such a sacrifice.

ROLLS-ROYCE

WRAITH

THE WRAITH COUPÉ MEASURES 5.3 METRES FROM NOSE TO TAIL, WEIGHS 2.5 TONNES, COSTS £215,000 and boasts a single pair of enormous 'suicide' doors. Under that huge bonnet is a 6.0-litre twin-turbo V12 engine churning out 600bhp. This is not, by any measure, a car for shrinking violets. But once you've got to grips with the pitch and sheer scale of the Wraith, it's the little details that really take your breath away. This car is a masterwork of craftsmanship.

Its dash clock is a miniature art-deco masterpiece, the vents are works of sculpture in their own right (not to mention capable of blasting out air with enough violence to severe hand from wrist). The indicator is the slenderest of spindles, daftly delicate within the gargantuan proportions of the car. Each door card is a single, immaculate slab of wood, four foot across by two foot high. The Wraith's shagpile floor mats are deep enough to permanently

devour feet. The 'Starlight' headlining, which sees some 1300 LED lights hand-woven into the roof, might sound like an add-on too garish for even the most taste-deficient Premiership reprobate, but in reality is entirely soothing and lovely.

But the Wraith is the first Rolls in decades – arguably ever – in which you're more likely to find the owner behind the wheel rather than lounging on the back seat, devouring peeled grapes and laughing at poor people. Rolls-Royce describes the Wraith as the most dynamic car in its history, which is admittedly rather like being heralded as the fleetest-footed national museum. Yes, the Wraith does feel more dynamic than the Phantom, or indeed any other Rolls. But by any conventional metric, this thing is still vast and lightly terrifying. Oh, it's fast (0–62mph takes 4.4 seconds, top speed is necessarily limited to 155mph), but the Wraith seems to regard hands-on driving – wrestling the

wheel, exploring the limits of grip – as rather uncouth. There's no faddish Sport button, no paddles to override the gear changes from the seven-speed auto box, which analyses GPS and sat-nav data to determine the most appropriate gear for the next corner. The message is clear: don't concern yourself with such menial tasks as changing gear, sir. The Rolls shall do that for you.

The twin-turbo 6.0-litre V12 keeps you at arm's length, too. This might be the only car in the world to make 600bhp feel comfortable, adequate, rather than obscene. Sure, the Wraith is rapid, but never uncivilly so: an elegant sufficiency of power, more than sir should ever need deploy. Which isn't to say you can't make progress, as the Rolls community might have it. Once you get that enormous, schooner-like nose pointed at the exit of a corner, you can call up all that power and surf you way out on a wave of imperial British torque. But try to drive it like an Elise, chuck the

big girl around, and you'll find the Wraith gives a polite cough and mutters, 'I think not, old chap.' Smoothly does it, that's the way.

Dynamic it may be, but the Wraith still floats with superlative … Rollsishness, silent and serene even at silly speeds, with a shag-pile ride to match its carpets. True, it's a mite firmer than its Rolls brethren: you occasionally get the slightest hint, through the seat or steering wheel, that you might have bumped over something fairly significant. A rhino, perhaps. But compared to anything but its big brother, the Phantom, the Wraith is as silky as motoring gets.

Back in the old days, the company used to boast that, at 60mph, the loudest noise you could hear from the driver's seat of a Rolls was the ticking of the clock. Things have changed today, but not a whole lot. At motorway speeds in the Wraith, you can't hear even the clock ticking. The only sound is that of expensive, deafening silence.

JAGUAR
F-TYPE

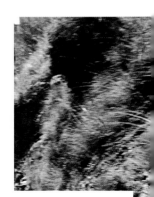

IN 1961, JAGUAR REVEALED THE E-TYPE. It was quite simply the most knee-tremblingly gorgeous car the world had ever seen. Even Enzo Ferrari, widely lauded as one of the grumpiest men in the history of motoring, described it as the most beautiful car in the world.

And then, having created the most jaw-dropping sports car on the planet, Jaguar sort of … forgot how to. For about half a century. Sure, there were fast Jaguars, and there were pretty Jaguars, but none truly recaptured the spirit and style of the original E-Type.

But then, in 2013, after years of teasing and hint-dropping, Jaguar unleashed the F-Type, a two-seat, rear-wheel-drive cabrio that invoked all of its predecessor's 1960s cool, a masterpiece of design culminating in one of the best backsides in automotive history. But under the F-Type's sleek exterior lurks a truly hairy-

chested sports car. And on a slippery British road on a slippery British winter's night, it isn't a car for the faint-hearted. It's an old-school hot rod of a drive, the F-Type, ready to bite if you show it the slightest sign of disrespect. Unlike, say, the Porsche Cayman, which is always on your side, the F-Type will happily spit you into a roadside ditch if you treat it without sufficient deference.

The engines are decidedly hirsute, too. Though the supercharged V6 F-Type is perhaps the sweetest drive in the line-up, the range-topping 500bhp V8 is the most addictive, not so much for its extra pace as the insane soundscape that emerges from its quad exhausts: a mix of *Saving Private Ryan* gunshot barrage and the ripping, metallic shriek of a buzz-saw slicing through a mains gas pipe.

It's a long way from perfect, the F-Type. With a spare tyre on board, there's approximately enough bootspace for a travel toothbrush, a pair of socks and, well, that's about it. But, hey, it's beautiful, and British, and frankly what more do you need?

McLAREN

P1

TALK ABOUT A DIFFICULT SECOND ALBUM. MCLAREN'S FIRST-EVER ROAD CAR WAS THE EPOCHAL F1 OF 1992, a three-seat hypercar that utterly redefined the world's conception of 'fast'. The F1 clocked 240mph in an era when 200mph was considered the very limit of speed, a production car record that stood until 2005, when the Bugatti Veyron reached 253mph. But it was more than just a speed freak: the F1 is widely regarded as one of the finest driver's cars of all time. In album terms, it was *Pet Sounds*, *London Calling* and *Sgt Pepper's Lonely Hearts Club Band* all rolled into one.

So un-follow-up-able was the F1 that it took McLaren fully 21 years – and every last gram of its Formula One know-how – to finalize its hypercar successor, warming up with a mere supercar in the shape of the 12C. Perhaps wisely, McLaren didn't set out to make the P1 faster than its predecessor, nor indeed the Bugatti Veyron. Instead, it modestly pitched the P1 as 'the best driver's car in the world, on road and track'.

You know what? It just might be. Provided, that is, you're a very, very good driver.

The P1 is built around a heavily altered version of the 3.8-litre V8 twin-turbo from its little brother, the 12C. This makes a vast 727bhp, the sort of figure most hypercars would consider more than enough. But not the P1, which also employs an electric motor making 176bhp and 192lb·ft of torque – double the output of the KERS system in 2013's F1 cars, no less – that neatly fills the holes in the turbo engine's torque curves. Yes, this thing is a hybrid, but one that hijacks green technology in the pursuit of speed.

That said, you can, should the mood take you, drive the P1 in all-electric mode for seven miles or so. But the mood far likelier to take you is to slip the P1 into maximum-attack 'Race' mode, which serves up the full 903bhp

through the rear wheels. You'd best be on your game when you do so. The P1 isn't just ludicrously fast – 0–62mph in 2.8 seconds and a limited top speed of 217mph, officially – but as sharp-edged as a suitcase of freshly whetted samurai swords. It corners like an F1 car, will spin its wheels right the way through fourth gear, and will chuck you many miles into the distant scenery if you exceed your reserves of driving talent by even a micrometre. This is a car even racing drivers will struggle to exploit to its full potential.

The P1 is born of motorsport, and demonstrates the fastidious attention to detail of McLaren's F1 operation. It is packed with added lightness: the entire chassis weighs just 90kg, while the windscreen is just 3.2mm thick, and 3.5kg lighter than the 12C's 'screen. The carbon ceramic brakes are impregnated with something called silicone carbide, used on the Ariane rocket programme for its heat-resistant properties.

The aerodynamics are equally boggling. Between its venturis, vents, wings and apertures, the P1 makes 600kg of downforce at 160mph: equivalent to the weight of an F1 car flattening it to the tarmac. The vast rear wing can flip up to provide extra brake force, or retract flat in just half a second to reduce aero drag when you're on a top-speed run. In fact, so much force does that spoiler produce that, at speeds over 156mph, it actually flattens itself off a little to prevent the sheer downforce snapping the suspension. The P1 produces 'ground effect' – a vacuum below the car – like a Le Mans racer, sucking it to the road. Even Clarkson struggled to get his head round the speed and sheer cleverness of McLaren's hybrid masterpiece.

'We have never encountered anything quite like the P1,' said JC when he tested the McLaren round Belgium's fearsome Spa circuit. 'This takes our perception of speed to a new level. You have about four heart attacks and six adrenaline surges every ten seconds…'

GERMANY

There is much debate over which nation first laid its towel on the car-building deckchair, but the strongest claim is staked by Karl Benz in the German city of Mannheim in the late 1880s. Never a nation to squander an advantage, since that time Germany has been working overtime to perfect the car formula, stopping only occasionally for a well-earned bratwurst and hot lap of the Nurburgring. If it's precision engineering you want, look no further than Germany. When Teutonic engineers set out to solve a problem – be it turning hybrid power into ultimate speed in the shape of the Porsche 918, or discovering precisely how many horsepowers you can pump into a family estate without creating a small black hole and destroying Europe (that's you, Audi RS6) – they generally come up with a mighty convincing, mighty fast answer.

PORSCHE
CARRERA GT

'THIS IS THE MOST EXCITING, THE BEST-LOOKING, THE MOST EXPENSIVE AND THE FASTEST ROAD-GOING PORSCHE EVER MADE,' declared Clarkson when he tested the Carrera GT back in 2004.

And though the mid-engined, rear-wheel-drive V10 supercar has since been usurped in at least some of those measures by its spiritual successor, the 918 Spyder, the Carrera GT still remains perhaps the most thrilling Porsche ever made. Or, as Jeremy put it rather more succinctly: 'Make a mistake in this and it'll kill you.'

The Carrera GT packed a 5.7-litre V10, originally designed by Porsche's motorsport team for endurance racing. It made a dizzying 612bhp at 8000rpm, which saw the flyweight, carbon fibre GT officially crack 0–62mph in 3.9 seconds – though Porsche has always been notoriously conservative with its acceleration figures – with a 205mph top speed.

'In even the fastest, most exotic cars there's a point that the power begins to lose its battle with the friction of the air, but with this … there's no let-up at all,' said Clarkson. 'It's like it's moving in a vacuum. It just isn't going to stop!'

And the Carrera GT boasted scalpel-edged handling to match its acceleration. 'This has no electronic overlord, nowhere to put your golf bags,' grimaced Clarkson as he wrestled the GT around Hammerhead. 'This is a car designed to go as fast as is technically possible. You need to be awake to drive this fast. It isn't an easy car to control, but if you put in the effort, boy oh boy do you get the rewards …'

True, the Carrera GT wasn't styled with the passion or verve of a Ferrari or Lamborghini. But it was, in its own minimalist way, entirely beautiful – a perfect example of form following function. 'It's so precise and elegant and focused,' cooed Clarkson.

The interior, too, was as focused as a very focused thing, all bare carbon and metal and even a very cool beechwood gear knob that paid homage to the shifters of Porsche's iconic, terrifying 917 Le Mans racers. The Carrera GT was as close as us mortals might ever come to that endurance-racing experience.

GUMPERT
APOLLO

'WHEN JEREMY TESTED THE ALFA 8C,' WINCED HAMMOND WHEN HE DROVE THE GUMPERT APOLLO, 'the camera crew found there wasn't a single angle that didn't make the car look brilliant. This is … the exact opposite. It's not exactly a looker.' Not only does the Apollo boast visuals only a mother could love, a £250,000 price tag and a name like a northern comedian, it also requires a degree in mechanical engineering to operate. You can adjust its camber, ride height, spring tensions and anti-roll bars, which is all very good if you're James May, but for the rest of us means you're likely to make your very expensive, very ugly hypercar irredeemably worse to drive. Even the traction control isn't a simple on-off switch, but rather a dial with which you can select the precise percentage of electronic assistance you require. 'Quite a lot' is the correct answer.

However, the Apollo does have a few redeeming features. For a start, it employs a 4.2-litre V8 engine sourced from Audi, but with added twin turbos for added goodness. You can have it in race-spec 800bhp trim, 700bhp for the road, or – if you've just passed your driving test, an 'entry level' 650bhp. None are exactly slow: the 700bhp version will go from nought to 62mph in three seconds dead and all the way to 224mph.

The reason this thing looks like the boil on the buttock of a baboon is because every hole, wing and slash is there to increase downforce. The Apollo glues itself to the road at speed, allowing you to corner at phenomenal, face-reshaping pace. In the hands of His Stigness, the Apollo hurled itself round the *Top Gear* test track in a time of 1m17.1s, just a couple of milliseconds slower than the Bugatti Veyron Super Sport, the official Fastest Car on the Planet. That's very, very fast. If you want a supercar you can park with pride in Monte Carlo's Casino square, this isn't the car for you. But on a race-track, the Apollo will destroy almost every car alive.

AUDI
R8 V10

WHEN AUDI ANNOUNCED PLANS FOR A SUPERCAR TO RIVAL FERRARI, LAMBO AND PORSCHE, MANY ASSUMED THE RESULT WOULD BE – NOT TO PUT TOO FINE A POINT ON IT – A PILE OF CODSWALLOP. After all, Audi mainly made cars for German cement salesmen: reliable, sensible, more than a little dull. Could the straightest-laced of Germany's straight-laced manufacturers possibly produce a car with the soul to match the best of Italy and the rest of the world?

In a word, yes. 'As far as I'm concerned, this car is almost without fault,' gushed Clarkson when he first tested the R8. Made from a blend of carbon fibre, magnesium and aluminium, and powered by a 4.2-litre V8, the R8 serves up genuinely enervating acceleration … and even goes round corners. 'Driving most supercars,' according to Clarkson, 'is like trying to manhandle a cow up a back staircase. This is like smearing honey over Keira Knightley. As a driver's car, this is spectacularly good.' And despite ticking all the supercar design boxes –

low, wide, angry – the R8 is even passably practical, too. There's a usable boot at the front, and enough space inside to move about. And breathe.

A pretty perfect effort, then. But then Audi went and made the R8 a little bit more perfect, stuffing it with a 5.2-litre V10 borrowed from Lamborghini, an engine with 518bhp and enough torque to tenderize an elephant. Which created a car not only supercar-fast – nought to 62mph in 3.7 seconds and a top speed knocking on the door of 200mph – but, with four-wheel drive, one that lets you access all that speed everywhere, all the time. Not only can you blitz the R8 to the rev limiter on tarmac, requiring a ginger right foot in a rear-wheel-drive supercar, but it sounds ruddy marvellous when you do. Job done, Audi. In fact, the only thing Clarkson could find to criticize was those LED front lights, which, according to the big man, 'make it look like a council house at Christmas'. Some people are just impossible to please, aren't they?

VOLKSWAGEN

SCIROCCO

VOLKSWAGEN'S 'NEW BEETLE' IS A VILE
ABOMINATION OF A CAR: an unfaithful rehash, a cynical
attempt to cash in on the happy-clappy, flowers-in-your-hair
vibe of the Nazi-engineered original; a car that – though hated
by many, including one J. Clarkson – was a genuine trendsetter
in its day. And, on paper, the Scirocco should be more of the
same. Like the new Beetle, it's a slab of retro that shamelessly
references one of VW's biggest hits from its back catalogue
– in this case the firm's Golf-based seventies coupé. Like the
Beetle, the new Scirocco sits on Golf underpinnings and, like
the Beetle, it trades in practicality for old-school looks.

But, unlike the Beetle, the Scirocco is brilliant. It retains
the free spirit of its original, but injects it with the quality
underpinnings of the irritatingly good modern Golf. Though
you can have it with a fizzy 1.4-litre petrol or even a diesel,
the Scirocco you want is the 'GT', which uses the punchy
2.0-litre petrol from the Golf GTI. With this engine, the
Scirocco will accelerate from nought to 60 in just under
seven seconds, and keep running to nearly 150mph. Fast
without being truly blistering, then, but the Scirocco makes
up for its modest output with a deliciously crisp drive.

It feels very much like a Golf GTI, only honed a fraction
in every regard. Sure-footed, accurate, bags of grip, it does
everything you ask of it. And because you sit lower in the
Scirocco, wrapped within its coupé shape, it feels somehow faster
than the Golf. But even if it drove like a rusty shed, we'd still love
the Scirocco. Because … just look at it. This is a sensible, practical
car you might realistically choose as an alternative to, say, a three-
door Renault Mégane, but visually it's far more special than that.
The Scirocco is a car that manages to look both retro and modern
at the same time: a tough trick to pull off. Just ask the new Beetle.

KTM
X-BOW

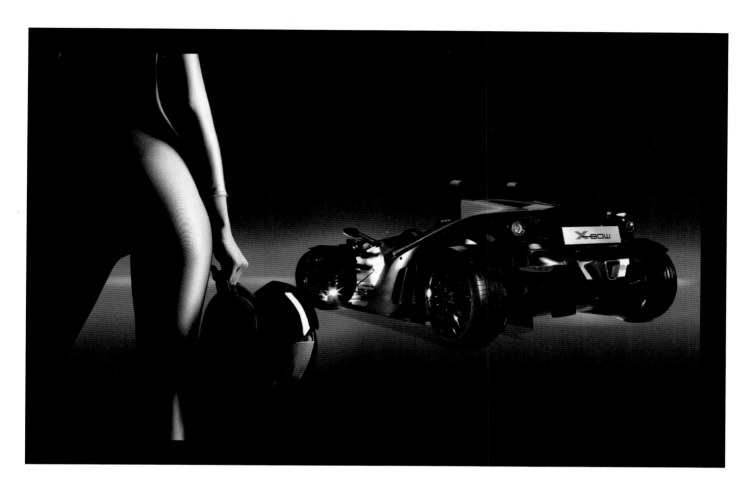

LEATHER CLOTHING ENTHUSIASTS WILL KNOW KTM AS A BIG NAME IN THE WORLD OF MOTORCYCLES. But, before the X-Bow (officially pronounced 'Cross-Bow', apparently), the Austrian manufacturer had never made a car before. Not a bad place to start, eh?

It's an extraordinary-looking thing, the X-Bow, all air-funnelling blades and slats and bare carbon, topped off with a pair of mirror pods that give this road-legal lightweight the unsettling appearance of a giant robot wasp sent from the future to enslave us all. It's a design that makes the similarly no-frills Ariel Atom look a trifle … unfinished, and the Caterham R500 look like a product of the 1950s. Which, erm, it is.

The race-grade goodness continues inside (if, indeed, the word 'inside' can be applied to a car with no roof and no doors. There's a race-spec LCD display, a pedal box that slides fore and aft, and a removable steering wheel. Even the X-Bow's seats are minimalist masterpieces, little more than a scrap of padding glued to a carbon fibre shell fixed within the monocoque.

On paper, then, the X-Bow sounds as hardcore as they come. But here's the thing. It isn't. Despite an absence of antilock brakes or traction control, this is a soft-edged puppy of a lightweight, its sharp edges meticulously smoothed off. It's easy to drive fast – almost too easy – and utterly unintimidating. Its engine, a modest 2.0-litre turbo sourced from Audi, makes 237bhp and its maximum 229lb·ft of torque at a very un-race-car 2000rpm.

Which makes the X-Bow, for something that looks like it should be starring in Michael Bay's *Transformers* franchise, a – relatively – comfortable thing in which to cover long distances. OK, there's not much in the way of weather protection – unless you go for the optional wraparound windscreen, which you must not because it makes the KTM look like a cartoon dog wearing sunglasses – but with the weather set fair, you could happily countenance the prospect of a cross-continent jaunt in this thing. Provided you're not bringing any luggage. Sharp-edged the KTM might look, but this is as cuddly as track-focused lightweights get.

MERCEDES-BENZ

CLK AMG
BLACK

JEREMY CLARKSON, AS YOU MAY HAVE NOTICED, IS NOT AN EASY MAN TO IMPRESS. In fact, Jeremy Clarkson is a man who could stumble over an unclaimed winning Euromillions ticket and still complain about the fact he had to bend down to pick it up. But in the face of the Mercedes CLK Black – the even-more-hardcore version of AMG's hardcore super-coupé – even JC could find nothing of which to complain.

'Here is the only car I know which really does achieve the impossible,' enthused Clarkson when he tested it in Wales. 'A car that could quite happily get you, and more luggage than you could imagine, to Beijing. But which, I imagine, could happily bite chunks out of a Porsche 911 Turbo's arse on a twisting a deserted piece of Welsh A-road.'

High praise indeed from the big man. But then the CLK Black is quite a car. It saw the CLK AMG's screaming 6.2-litre V8 bumped up past 500bhp courtesy of a new exhaust and electronics, along with an almost pathological diet strategy. The CLK's posh seats were replaced with body-hugging buckets, while the sat nav, back seats and many of the airbags were chucked out. Even the door panels were rendered in carbon fibre. All of which meant ... the Black weighed just a little bit more than when the AMG engineers started.

Why? Because of a vast new rear axle and differential to cope with the extra power. Which the CLK Black did admirably. 'Initially it scares you half to death, because it seems to be dancing down the road,' said Clarkson. 'And then you realize it is dancing. You're just telling it where to go.'

OK, so JC did manage to find one fault: that the CLK Black cost £34,000 more than the standard AMG CLK, a rather cynical interpretation of the 'less is more' ethos. But beyond that, Clarkson was stumped. 'The Black is brilliant, everywhere, at absolutely everything,' he eulogized. 'I shall doff my cap to anyone who buys one.'

Presumably some furious self-doffing followed not long after. Clarkson loved the CLK Black so much that he bought one.

WHEN AUDI UNVEILED THE TT IN 1998, IT CHUCKED A HAND GRENADE INTO THE COSY WORLD OF CAR DESIGN. The crisp, minimalist coupé achieved instant acclaim as a design icon, instantly making almost everything else on the road look bloated and overwrought.

But despite its visual impact, the TT became quickly – and perhaps a little unfairly – known as a 'hairdresser's car', a coupé for those who preferred to waft around and look good rather than actually, y'know, drive. A more-than-slightly soggy Golf in a spangly shirt.

The TT-RS changed all that. The hottest version of the second-generation TT, the RS finally gave the TT the bite to match its visual flair.

Forget some boosted-up, common-as-muck four cylinder, the TT-RS got a unique, exotic new engine: a turbo five cylinder sending a juicy 340bhp to all four wheels. It was a powertrain that sang of Audi's fast car history: the original Quattro – square

arches, World Rally Championship, Pikes Peak, Walter Röhrl – used a turbo five too. Hardly a hairdressing history, that.

And, like its rallying forebear, this thing accelerates like it's on a mission. It's not just the 4.6-second 0–62mph time – though that's serious sports-car territory in itself – but the full-on turbo boost it serves up from deep down in the rev range, giving you an instant slug of power wherever and whenever you need it.

The TT-RS is a proper terrier for corners, too: all you, as the driver, have to do is chuck it in and let the four-wheel drive sort it out. No, it doesn't have quite the delicacy of, say, a Porsche Cayman, but you can invest huge trust in the TT and the grip it provides. It feels, in many ways, like a mini-Veyron: fast, full of boost, almost impossible to unstick.

It's a trifle more wieldy – not to mention cheaper – than that Bugatti, too. With that turbo five up front, the nose feels pointy, the TT emitting a delicious, eighties-style warble as it thumps itself at its redline. The only haircut this coupé is dishing out is a buzzcut skinhead …

AUDI

TT-RS

MERCEDES McLAREN
SLR STIRLING MOSS

IN 1955, BRITISH RACING GREAT SIR STIRLING MOSS – WIDELY REGARDED AS THE FINEST DRIVER NEVER TO WIN AN F1 TITLE – took an astonishing victory in the Mille Miglia, Italy's insane endurance road race, in a Mercedes 300 SLR. Moss and navigator Denis Jenkinson covered the thousand-mile road loop in just over ten hours, at an average speed of 98mph.

In celebration of this achievement, a mere 54 years later, Mercedes and McLaren cooked up a roofless, ridiculous hypercar in honour of Sir Stirling's improbable feat: a roofless, ridiculous hypercar that also gave the firms' joint SLR project a fitting send-off.

It was a send-off designed to put the McMerc's fearsome 5.4-litre supercharged V8 centre-stage, with no roof or glass to impede the fury of its 650 horsepowers coursing to the rear wheels, and the noise coursing from under the bonnet and from the side-exit exhaust. Outside Formula One, it's hard to think of

a car that offers a more dramatic view from the driver's seat than the SLR Stirling Moss, with no windscreens nor pillars (a pair of tiny wind deflectors are all that protect the Moss's occupants from onrushing bees) to obscure the vista. The cabin is 1950s-minimal: just a couple of vents, two seats, a gear lever … and that's about it.

Weighing a giant 200kg less than the SLR Coupé, and with a 0–62mph time of 3.5 seconds and top speed around 217mph, there's only one way to describe driving the Moss: terrifying. The roofless SLR launches off the line with the noise and fury of a Saturn 5 rocket on take-off, and accrues speed with a force that's physically painful as the wind whips your face. Corners? Not so much. As Hunter S. Thompson said of the Vincent Black Shadow bike: 'It's not much for turning, but it's pure hell on the straightaway.'

Biblically fast and utterly terrifying? A fitting tribute to Sir Stirling's Italian escapades …

BMW
M3 GTS

IN 2010, THE BMW M3 CELEBRATED ITS 25TH ANNIVERSARY. But how to say happy birthday to one of the most iconic sports cars of recent times?

With a new, £120,000, no-expense-spared M3, that's how. Which is, admittedly, a stupendous sum of money for a car that is, at the end of the day, still just a 3-Series. But the M3 was so astoundingly good, and did its stuff in such a barnstormingly unique way, that it was almost – almost – worth the money.

For a start, it looks mean enough to give passers-by a black eye just for staring at it: black lightweight alloys, adjustable rear spoiler nicked from BMW's world touring car team, new cooling ducts and a front splitter extendable by 30mm for extra downforce.

And it sounds as mean as it looks. The 4.4-litre V8 – much more than a breathed-on version of the normal M3's engine, instead a bespoke motorsport unit making a heady 444bhp – erupts into life before settling to a race-car idle, lumpy and grumpy and uneven. It sounds like something that means business, and, as you wring it out to its 8500rpm redline, it morphs into a cylinder-packed din that's a bit scary and absolutely bloody marvellous.

And to drive? Like an M3, only 200 per cent more M3-ish. The GTS feels tight as a drum, with no hint of slack. Depending on your mood, it can trace the perfect arc through a tricky corner, or demolish it in a tyre-immolating bout of oversteer.

Beware rain. Ultra-precise it may be in the dry, but on a wet road, the rear-drive GTS feels decidedly … wayward. With the stability systems turned on it won't quite let go completely, but this is a tail-happy, bad-ass BMW from the old school.

Worth £120,000? Well, with just 126 ever built – of which just 8 made their way to the UK – the GTS has guaranteed status as a gold-plated future classic. With the 2014 M3 going turbocharged, this was a worthy swansong for the naturally aspirated M-car.

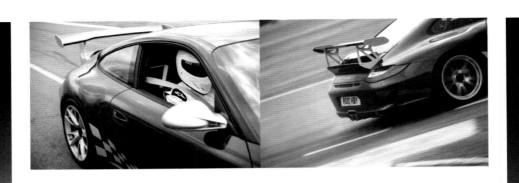

PORSCHE
911 GT3 RS

THE 911 GT3 IS PRETTY MUCH AS RAZOR-TIPPED AS A ROAD CAR CAN GET, but for a company as anal about engineering as Porsche, 'pretty much' isn't enough. As a final hurrah for the '997' generation 911, before it was replaced by the '991' series and its all-new engine, Porsche took its hardcore GT3 and put it on a crash diet.

So the GT3 RS is 25kg lighter than the already anorexic 911 GT3, a weight saving achieved through an almost pathological determination to shave grams anywhere and everywhere possible. The single-mass flywheel is 1.4kg lighter, the brake hubs are aluminium and save 1.2kg a corner. The rear window is plastic, the door handles are canvas straps and the gearbox is an old-school, lightweight manual. A massive carbon fibre rear wing helps the RS generate as much downforce at 100mph as the standard GT3 does at 190.

With the venerable Metzinger 3.8-litre flat-six engine pumping out 444bhp through the rear wheels, this is one of the most visceral cars on the road. You don't so much sit in the RS as become plugged into its ECU, with no frilly stuff between what you do and what the car does. This is pure mechanical engineering, the RS emitting a delicious, industrial array of whirrs, gasps and clatters. Every control is perfectly balanced: flex your toe by the tiniest amount and the RS3 leaps forward like a just-branded cow: 0–62mph takes four seconds flat, with top speed standing at 192mph.

There are downsides. At idle, the RS's flyweight flywheel rattles like a tin of nails, and the interior lacks, well … anything. Oh, and the GT3 RS costs £106,000, which is an awful lot of money for an intentionally very small amount of 911. But for a sports car this good, it's a bargain. And to think this thing started its life, once upon a time, as a VW Beetle …

BMW

1M

THE BMW 1M IS LIKE A TURKEY CURRY ON BOXING DAY. It's made from leftovers. To create this muscular micro-coupé, BMW took a standard 1-Series, pumped it up a bit and added some spare parts it had lying around: the door mirrors from the current M3, the rear axle from the last one, the engine from a Z4.

It's a recipe that shouldn't work, but it does. Spectacularly. Hodge-podge the 1M might be, but it's also one of the finest little sports cars of the last few decades. 'I haven't driven anything this perfect since the original Golf GTI,' grinned Clarkson as he slid the 1M around the *Top Gear* test track. 'It just feels so beautifully balanced…'

There's nothing especially exotic on the 1M ingredients list. That Z4 straight-six is boosted to 340bhp with the aid of a pair of turbochargers, and drives the rear wheels through a simple six-speed manual gearbox. Simple, yes, but a simple recipe for a car quick enough to out-drag a Porsche Cayman and Lotus Evora over a quarter-mile race: one that'll officially manage the 0–62mph run in 4.9 seconds and has to be limited to a 155mph maximum.

And it's a car with a penchant for big, smoky drifts. 'Just when you think it can't possibly get any better, you push the little M button on the steering wheel and the whole car shimmers … a little shiver of excitement,' said Clarkson as he engulfed the TG circuit in clouds of immolated rubber. 'In M mode it's even more of a tyre-smoker.'

And because the 1M is, at heart, a humble 1-Series, there's space in the back for two children, and room in the boot for two more. It's a family coupé, but one with the ability to vanquish sports cars. 'This does to today's sports cars what the original Golf GTI did to the MG and the Triumph Spitfire,' reckoned JC. 'It renders them … pointless.'

Issues? Not many. True, the 1M rides a little hard, but, as Clarkson puts it: 'You won't notice the stiff suspension because you'll be having such a good time. This is a brilliant, brilliant, brilliant car. The end.'

BUGATTI
VEYRON SS

FOR MOST COMPANIES, CREATING THE FASTEST PRODUCTION CAR IN HISTORY – ONE THAT STRETCHED THE VERY LIMITS OF AUTOMOTIVE POSSIBILITY IN THE TWENTY-FIRST CENTURY, one that did for cars what Concorde did for air travel in the 1970s – would be enough. But not for the mighty Volkswagen empire and its all-conquering 1,000bhp Bugatti Veyron.

After all, 2005's Veyron achieved all it set out to achieve. It smashed the production car speed record into smithereens, clocking 254mph at VW's Ehra-Lessien test track, a quantum leap beyond the McLaren's existing mark of 240mph. With four-wheel drive, broadly idiot-proof handling and a comfy, leathery cabin, it put 1,000bhp within the reach of drivers of sub-Stig-spec talent. It spirited Jeremy from Italy to London faster than Hammond and May in a plane. What more, frankly, could a car achieve?

But then those pesky Americans at SSC took their Ultimate Aero to 256mph in 2007, nicking the production speed record from the Veyron. Other companies would have shrugged, accepted that records are there to be broken, and gone back to playing golf or maypole dancing or whatever it is that German engineers do in their downtime. But the VW empire doesn't really do 'shrugging' or 'accepting', and thus it was decided that something must be done to put those upstart Yankees back in their box.

That 'something' was the Veyron SuperSport, a car designed to demonstrate that the Bugatti engineers had taken it easy with the standard, left a bit in the tank. A car designed to go beyond 260mph.

But adding even a few miles an hour of extra speed to a car operating as close to the very edge of physics as the Veyron isn't easy. Because, as James May has often attempted to explain, aerodynamic drag increases exponentially as speed increases. Upping top speed is like compressing a coil spring: the effort is always doubling, and the contraction is always halving. So an extra 200bhp was required for a piffling top speed increase of 5mph.

Power from the Veyron's gargantuan 8.0-litre, 16-cylinder twin-turbo powerplant was upped by 200bhp to a pleasingly round 1,200 horsepowers, courtesy of bigger turbos, bigger intercoolers and a new exhaust. The bodywork was altered, too, with a new nose, engine cover and radically different intakes to shove more air to the monster furnace. Thanks to more liberal use of carbon fibre, the SuperSport was 50kg lighter than the (admittedly not especially light) Veyron.

Such fettling produced arguably the most astonishing set of statistics ever boasted by a licence-plate-wearing car. The Veyron SuperSport costs around £2,000,000 after taxes, will haul from nought to 62mph in something like 2.3 seconds and on to 124mph just 4.4 seconds later. At full chat, it burns 7.7 litres of fuel every minute, thus emptying its giant fuel tank in just eight minutes. The tyres that can cope with the insane speed served up by the SuperSport are so advanced that they cost £20,000 a set. That pop-up rear wing acts as an airbrake that can generate 0.7g of stopping power alone.

Yet the Veyron SS's most astounding trick is that it manages to make 1,200bhp feel acceptable, usable. Around town, the big Bug, with its double-clutch gearbox, is as docile as an automatic VW Golf (albeit a trifle wider), with a spacious, cool interior and simple controls. But find a very, very long runway and you'll discover a car that accelerates beyond the limit of human comprehension, that continues hauling and hauling when even the very fastest cars on the planet have run out of puff.

How fast exactly? Well, in the hands of James May on Ehra-Lessien's 5.5-mile straight, the Veyron SuperSport clocked a ridiculous 259mph, wrestling the speed crown back from the Germans and making Captain Slow the fastest man ever in a production car. And then, ten minutes later, Bugatti's test driver Pierre-Henri Raphanel went out in the SS and hit 268mph, thus handing James May the least-amount-of-time-holding-a-world-record record. Permission to say 'Oh cock' …

BMW

M550d

BIG DIESEL SALOONS SHOULD HAVE NO PLACE ON A LIST OF THE DREAM CARS OF THE TWENTY-FIRST CENTURY. But we'll make an exception for a big diesel saloon that's packing a pummelling 546lb·ft of torque – or, to put it another way, double the twist of a Porsche Cayman.

That clubbing output comes courtesy of a triple turbo – because frankly *Top Gear* has always regarded two turbos as woefully insufficient – straight-six diesel,

one capable of hauling the M550d to 62mph in just 4.7 seconds and headlong into its 155mph limit.

In other words, this is a diesel 5-Series that will keep pace with an M5. Or an Aston Martin V8 Vantage. But even the M550d's awesome stats don't tell the true story: unlike most petrol engines, which don't make their full power until high revs, the big 5 serves up all its torque from a virtual standstill, meaning there's power on tap wherever and whenever you need it. And

with four-wheel drive, it can drive that power straight to the tarmac where the rear-wheel-drive M5 will be spinning its wheels.

And though such hairshirt considerations as economy and emissions have no place on a list of dream cars, it's worth noting that the M550d's quoted 55 miles per gallon will get well-heeled British skiists most of the way to their Alpine retreats before having to refuel: in that big, petrolly M5, they'd barely be past Calais before pulling into the filling station.

Does that make the M550d the perfect fast saloon, then? Not quite. At least, not if you live in Britain. Or Japan. Or Australia. Or Lincolnshire. Or any other country that drives on the left. Because, if you do, you can't have the M550d: at least, not with the wheel where it should be. BMW says the four-wheel-drive system gets in the way of flipping the steering wheel from left to right, so it'll only be offering the 550d in left-hand-drive markets. It's enough to have *Top Gear* considering emigration …

MERCEDES-BENZ

SLS BLACK

THE BLACK SERIES IS THE HARDER, FASTER, NASTIER VERSION OF MERCEDES'S BELLOWING, GULLWING SLS, a car few ever regarded as being lacking in the hard/fast/nasty department. It uses the same 6.2-litre V8 as the standard SLS, but revs to a dizzying 8000rpm, a redline jump of 800rpm. That giant powerplant now makes 622bhp, some 59bhp more than the stock car and good for a 0–62mph time of just 3.2 seconds and a top speed very, very close to 200mph.

But the SLS Black is as much about what's been taken away as what's been added. The whole car is 70kg lighter: among the body panels, only the doors remain the same as the standard SLS. The rest of the body has swollen to accommodate the wider tracks: the SLS Black is 13mm wider at the front and 26mm wider at the rear than the already none-too-narrow SLS. The tyres, too, are yet wider, and are wrapped around lightweight wheels.

It sounds like a recipe for utter terror, but somehow the Black is actually less scary than the standard SLS. Where that car occasionally becomes puckeringly wayward, the Black Series feels utterly locked down, gaining pace with a dense energy. There's no slop between right foot and rear wheels, the whole car feeling taut and utterly free of slack. For a machine of its sheer heft, the SLS feels surprisingly agile, turning quickly and decisively. Of course, you must never forget that this is a big, front-engined, rear-drive brute: there's a lot of weight sitting over the front wheels, and it will delightedly engage in great lurid powerslides if you're that way inclined.

But the rest of the time, the SLS Black does a fine impression of a pin-sharp supercar, doing exactly what you ask of it without answering back, the gearbox slamming home every shift with ruthless efficiency. It might look like a no-holds-barred racer, but this is simply one of the best road cars of the century so far.

PORSCHE
BOXSTER

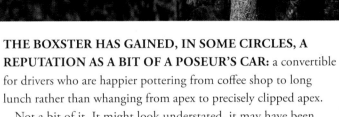

THE BOXSTER HAS GAINED, IN SOME CIRCLES, A REPUTATION AS A BIT OF A POSEUR'S CAR: a convertible for drivers who are happier pottering from coffee shop to long lunch rather than whanging from apex to precisely clipped apex.

Not a bit of it. It might look understated, it may have been cruelly christened 'the Coxster' by that reprobate Clarkson, but this dinky mid-engined roadster is arguably the best-driving open-top car you can buy.

Here's the operating procedure when driving a Boxster for the first time. 1) Approach driver's door. 2) Wriggle down into low, low driving seat. 3) Fire up 3.4-litre boxer engine. 4) Drop roof. 5) Press Sport and Noisy Exhaust buttons. 6) Commence driving. 7) Negotiate first corner. 8) Immediately consider what to sell, steal or embezzle to have this in your life permanently. Truly, it's that good.

There's nothing revolutionary in the Boxster's blueprint: a flat-six engine of natural aspiration and modest power mounted in the middle and driving the rear wheels. But it's a blueprint that is,

quite literally, perfectly balanced. When you drive the Boxster, it's almost impossible to discern where the mass of the engine lies: so perfectly sorted is that chassis that you simply don't notice the suspension doing its thing. However hard you lean on the Boxster, there's no sensation of weight transferring anywhere, just perfect poise and neutrality. Most drivers would go a whole lot faster in a Mitsubishi Evo, but have far more fun in a Boxster.

It's a masterwork of packaging, too. Find a friend who's not into cars, show them a Boxster and ask them to find the engine. Chances are they'll probably check the front boot first, but under that bonnet is just a decent-sized luggage space. The rear boot? Nope, another modest hole for more luggage. The Boxster's flat-six is tucked way down below the roof mechanism, somewhere just behind your buttocks.

Indeed, so irreproachable is the Boxster that it asks some mighty searching questions of its own big brother: the Porsche 911 cabriolet. Nothing like a healthy bit of family rivalry …

AUDI

RS6

AVANT

OF ALL THE ASTONISHING NUMBERS TO EMERGE FROM THE ASTONISHING CARS OF THE TWENTY-FIRST CENTURY, there are few more quietly breathtaking than this one: the Audi RS6 Avant will accelerate from standstill to 62mph in 3.9 seconds. Under four seconds. In a nearly-two-tonne family estate. That's as fast as the Ferrari F40 ever managed, acceleration once the realm of only the wildest supercars, achieved by a big five-seat wagon with space in the boot for many dogs and suitcases.

And you know what? It feels it. Nothing short of an Ariel Atom can rival the RS6 for reducing you to a cackling maniac as you plant the throttle, spool up the 4.0-litre, 552bhp twin-turbo V8 and try your feeble best to wrap your faculties around the sensory overload enveloping you. Difference is, where the Atom experience eases up as you hit triple figures – metered by aerodynamics and your own desire not to become an integral part of the scenery – the RS6 just keeps pulling and pulling at the same ludicrous rate, all the way to 189mph if you remove the limiters, which you simply must.

With all its thumping 516lb·ft of torque available from a lowly 1750rpm all the way to 5500rpm, there's also not much else on the planet that makes B-road overtaking so dismissively simple as the RS6. Gap-throttle-done. Gap-throttle-done. Repeat until all traffic is vanquished. Even on damp roads caked in gravel and cow dung and fallen leaves, the RS6 gets from A to B, C, D and the rest of the alphabet at absurd pace.

With a four-wheel drive system that can send up to 70 per cent of torque to the front wheels or as much as 85 per cent to the rears, the RS6's reserves of traction are almost impossible to deplete. No matter what speed and what corner, no matter whether you slam on the brakes or stab the throttle, somehow the Audi's array of differentials and

electronic trickery sorts it out. It's a car that instils great reserves of misplaced confidence, the belief you can head into any bend at any pace and emerge intact, confidence that may evaporate the day you find yourself entering a blind hairpin at triple-figure speed and, shortly thereafter, airborne somewhere over Dunkirk. Physics can only be bent so far.

It isn't the most … engaging thing to drive. In fact, the RS6 feels like a very fine computer simulation of itself, imbuing you with an air of detached immortality on the road. It's a small price to pay for something that sounds this good. The RS6 makes a bonkers, air-bullying soundtrack, snorting its way to 5000rpm like a brace of industrial vacuum cleaners battling to the death, and snap-cracking on the overrun with enough volume to reduce any toddlers within a five-mile vicinity to tears. So disconcertingly violent is the RS6's exhaust, in fact, that you occasionally find yourself wondering if the rear diff has splintered straight through the boot floor.

There's more than a little, ahem, cosmetic enhancement to the Audi's aurals. Open the door (when stationary, preferably), rev the engine and you'll find a chunk of the noise has mysteriously disappeared, an indication of just how much of that sound is of less than organic origin. An editing trick it may be, but it's a mighty effective one.

All this speed and noise and fury is all the more astonishing because, under its bulge-arched exterior, the RS6 is actually a bit of a vegan. Compared to the previous generation RS6, it has shed 100kg thanks to lots of lightweight aluminium in its body, is more economical and – in unprecedented scenes at the German Horsepower Society – less powerful than the car it replaces, trading its predecessor's V10 for an Audi-tuned version of the V8 doing sterling service in the Bentley Conti GT. A V8 that – thanks to clever shutdown tech – becomes a four-cylinder under light load, no less. As green icons go, it sure beats a Prius …

MERCEDES-BENZ
S-CLASS

IF YOU WANT TO DISCOVER WHAT TECHNOLOGY SHALL GRACE THE NORMAL CARS OF THIS WORLD – the Focuses, the Golfs, the Astras – in a decade or so, you don't need a crystal ball. You just need to drive the newest Mercedes S-Class. Though history, each new generation of Merc's big limo has represented a great leap forward for car technology, and the latest edition is no different.

You want *Tomorrow's World*-spec tricks? Try the S-Class's freakish 'Magic Body Control'. Binocular-vision cameras in the windscreen will spot bumps in the road ahead, causing the fully active suspension to raise each wheel at the very moment the hump is due to meet the tyre. Really. This thing can lift its paws to make bumps disappear. And it works, too, turning the most broken road into a silken magic carpet.

And the S-Class can pretty well drive itself. Set the adaptive cruise control, take your feet from the pedals and your hands from the wheel and the S-Class will steer, slow, accelerate and stop to keep its place in its lane and a safe distance from the car in front. It's not quite an autonomous car – you have to touch the wheel every ten seconds or so to assure the Merc that you've not nodded off – but it's mighty close.

The sum total of all this technology is a car that eases the strain of driving better than anything else on earth. Yes, you can have it with a barnstorming V8 or V12 AMG engine, but in truth you don't need to: even the basest diesel is more than as fast as you'll never need. The S-Class isn't about getting to your destination first, but arriving more relaxed than you would in any other luxury limo. It's a complicated car that makes driving very simple.

PORSCHE

911
TURBO S

THE 911 TURBO S BOASTS A STRONG CLAIM TO THE CROWN OF QUICKEST CAR IN THE REAL WORLD.
Sure, the record books may herald the Bugatti Veyron and its 268mph top speed; the Pagani Huayra and BAC Mono may sit atop the TGTV Power Laps board; and, true, on an empty track or airstrip in the hands of His Stigness, these three might edge out the Turbo S. But on the road? The Veyron, astonishing achievement though it is, is too large, too heavy, too damn intimidating to take close to its limits on normal public lanes. The rear-drive Huayra and Mono, meanwhile, require a driver of superhuman skill to exploit their full potential if the tarmac's anything other than bone dry and perfectly smooth. With a real, normal driver on a real, normal road, there's little on earth to touch the four-wheel-drive Turbo S.

Packing a bi-turbo 3.8-litre flat-six, the Turbo S sends 553bhp and a ludicrous 553 torques to four very large tyres. That's some 30bhp and 37lb.ft more than the last-gen 911 Turbo S, which few regarded as underpowered or slow. The new car's 0-62mph time is officially quoted at 3.1 seconds, which is frankly silly for something with at least a nominal set of rear seats and a decent front boot.

This thing is ludicrously fast, everywhere, all of the time. Autobahn, B-road, gravel, rain, no matter: the Turbo S is the sort of car you step from after a drive – even a short one – thankful to still possess your licence. It is blindingly fast, not as a figure of speech but quite literally. Yes, this car actually blinds you. Human eyes cannot cope with the sheer force of detonating from a standstill past 60mph in three seconds, the Turbo S flinging itself off the line with a lot of noise and just a hint of wheelspin. Clench

your jaw, squint, gurn, it's all useless: as launch control bites, the windscreen starts to swim, the scenery closes in around you, and then all is a blur as the G-force squeezes your eyeballs' vital fluids in directions vital eyeball fluids really shouldn't go. It is addictive and unsettling, not acceleration in the traditional sense but something rawer: thrust, the sensation of a jet airplane on take-off, a relentless surge seemingly independent of tarmac and tyres.

There's much cleverness to keep all that acceleration heading in the right direction. The Turbo S employs rear-wheel steer, angling the rear wheels some 1.5 degrees either way: at speeds below 31mph against the fronts, to reduce the turning circle and increase agility; at over 50mph with the fronts, for better stability. As well as that fat rear wing, the Turbo S boasts the world's first variable front spoiler, a four-inch-deep rubber skirt that extends from the bottom lip of the front bumper in three sections. At low speeds it remains retracted, its side sections only unfurling as you pass 75mph. But in track-attack mode, the spoiler is fully extended, for both maximum downforce and maximum usefulness as a driveway snow shovel come winter.

It makes an extraordinary noise, too. No, the turbo six doesn't scream like a Ferrari V8, but has a unique soundtrack all of its own: a bassy, phasing hum at idle, like something out a 1970s sci-fi series, morphing into a barrage of cannonfire exhaust as you thump up through the gears. It's an engine that gives you options. Want to drive it like a naturally aspirated sports car, butting up against the 7200rpm rev limiter? Happy to oblige. Prefer to keep it low and lazy, to use that skull-crushing sledgehammer of torque from 2000rpm? No problem, sir. However you drive it, pretty much no other licence-plate-wearing car will get close …

B M W i 8

THE I8 LOOKS LIKE A VISITOR FROM PLANET FUTURE, AND WHAT'S UNDER THAT SPACE-AGE BODYWORK IS JUST AS BRILLIANTLY STRANGE. Its engine is a modest 1.5-litre three-cylinder turbo, which doesn't sound big enough to shift a pushbike, let alone a sports car. But in conjunction with an electric motor, this thing packs enough of a punch to keep pace with an Aston Martin V8 Vantage.

Yes, it's a hybrid. But while the i8 can play the tree-hugger, running in emissions-free, all-electric mode around town if you so desire, the reason it uses not one source of power but two isn't in a hunt for all-efficiency, but rather efficient fastness.

Quite a lot of fastness. That petrol engine – which feeds the rear wheels – makes 230bhp, while the electric motor driving the front wheels adds another 130bhp. Which means 360bhp in what is effectively a four-wheel-drive coupé weighing under 1500kg. Nought to 62mph? 4.5 seconds.

Such a complicated system might sound like a surefire set-up for a weird, disjointed driving experience, but the i8 drives as sweetly as a BMW M3, albeit rather differently. That modest kerbweight and low centre of gravity – thanks to the floor-mounted battery pack – give a wonderful eagerness to the steering, and though those tyres look skinny, grip is strong. No, it's not a smoky oversteerer to rival that Aston Martin, but this is a sports car for the real world. The two motors complement each other, too, the electric module providing instant torque from zero revs before the petrol engine wakes up to haul the i8 onwards.

Astonishingly, it even sounds pretty good. In 'Sport' mode, the exhaust note is electronically boosted, offering up a bass-heavy thrum that hardens nicely as you head to the redline. Oh, and it officially returns 113mpg and just 59g/km of CO_2. The hybrid-flavoured future might not be so bad after all …

MERCEDES-BENZ

A45 AMG

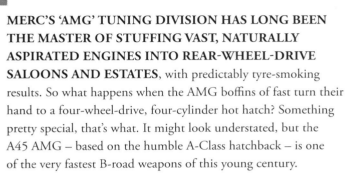

MERC'S 'AMG' TUNING DIVISION HAS LONG BEEN THE MASTER OF STUFFING VAST, NATURALLY ASPIRATED ENGINES INTO REAR-WHEEL-DRIVE SALOONS AND ESTATES, with predictably tyre-smoking results. So what happens when the AMG boffins of fast turn their hand to a four-wheel-drive, four-cylinder hot hatch? Something pretty special, that's what. It might look understated, but the A45 AMG – based on the humble A-Class hatchback – is one of the very fastest B-road weapons of this young century.

Under that bonnet is packed a 2.0-litre four-cylinder turbo petrol making a ridiculous 354bhp, giving the A45, says Merc, the highest 'power density' of any production engine. In other words, no other powerplant makes as many horsepowers per litre. For comparison, if the 8.4-litre Dodge Viper had the same power density, it'd make nearly 1500bhp.

That power is fed to all four wheels through a seven-speed dual-clutch gearbox, giving the A45 near-immutable traction and a real-world turn of pace to bother even some pretty serious supercars. Bury the throttle, wait for the turbo to spool up, and the A45 simply launches itself down the road, gripping on with the tenacity of an emotionally dependent limpet. The A45's four-wheel drive system is naturally front biased, only pushing power to the rear axle when it detects slip from the front wheels. So while it won't indulge in any sideways action, it's an easy, confidence-inspiring thing to drive on a damp country lane.

With the optional sports exhaust, the A45 sounds fabulous too, if perhaps not quite so mechanically pure as its huge-engined, naturally aspirated big brothers. Even so, the exhaust cracks, pops and whooshes with the addictive enthusiasm of a Group B rally car.

If you want a fizzy drive, the similarly potent, similarly compact but rear-drive BMW 1M might have the edge on the traction-tastic Merc. But for effortless, searing pace, there's little to match this A45.

VOLKSWAGEN
GOLF GTI

HISTORIANS DISAGREE WHETHER THE 1976 GOLF GTI WAS THE VERY FIRST HOT HATCH: SOME MAINTAIN IT WAS BEATEN TO THE CROWN BY THE SIMCA 1100 TI, A CAR, IT'S FAIR TO SAY, THAT HISTORY HAS TREATED RATHER LESS KINDLY THAN THE VW.

Whatever the back story, it's the Golf GTi that has, over nearly 40 years and 7 generations, become the archetypal hot hatch, the car that defines the breed. In its latest iteration, it's one of the most polished performers not only in the world of hot hatches, but fast cars as a whole.

VW has never worried about stuffing the Golf GTI with obscene amounts of power, content to leave the 276bhp Vauxhall Astra VXR and 265bhp Renault Mégane to their own torque-steery devices. In its latest iteration, the GTi makes a modest 218bhp from its 2.0 litre turbo petrol engine, though you can up it to 227bhp with the optional 'Performance Pack'. Whichever way, the VW lags well behind its hot-hatch rivals from Renault, Vauxhall and Ford in the horsepower stakes.

But what the Golf lacks in outright power, it makes up for by being the slickest, most fault-free hot hatch on the planet. Nothing else covers ground with quite the fuss-free pace of the GTi, shrugging off bumps, gripping hard no matter how wet, greasy or leaf-strewn the road. It's a car that flatters its driver, makes you feel you're smoother and neater than you really are.

The Golf doesn't concern itself with the huge wings, fat spoilers or lurid paintjobs of its showier rivals. This is a hot hatch from the subtle school, but the upgrades over the standard Golf are as smart as they are understated: neat red highlights, chunky flat-bottomed steering wheel, smart alloys and – if you go for the manual gearbox rather than the slick-shifting flappy-paddle transmission – a golf-ball style gearknob that pays homage to the shifter of the original Golf GTi.

Perhaps the GTi's only real flaw is that it's simply too polished. There's not a rough edge in sight anywhere here.

PORSCHE

918

PORSCHE TENDS TO DO THINGS PROPERLY. Purists might have grumbled when the world's premier purveyor of sports cars diversified into the world of 4x4s with the Cayenne, but there's no arguing that Porsche showed the world how to put the 'sport' into 'sport utility vehicle' with that car.

So when Porsche sets out to make a hybrid hypercar to rival the McLaren P1 and LaFerrari, a car combining the most baffling aspects of conventional and electric power, you can safely assume its engineers will do a thorough job. But the 918 is more than a decent first effort at a hybrid hypercar. It's an epoch-defining moment in the history of fast, packed with bleeding-edge technology that functions faultlessly and delivers truly brain-altering performance.

Here's how it works. In the middle of the 918's carbon chassis is a 4.6-litre V8, an engine borrowed from Porsche's racing division. On its own, it makes 603bhp, revs to a dizzying 9150rpm and weighs just 135kg. To that ample base, Porsche adds a pair of electric motors, one for each axle. These boost power to a rarefied 875bhp, and are fed from a battery pack mounted low in the car, their grunt reaching the wheels through a phenomenally complex array of differentials and software.

So what does all this complexity mean? Deranged, delicious speed. The 918 will do 0–60mph in 2.5 seconds, 0–125mph in 7.2 and 0–186mph in 20.9. Those are figures to rival the Veyron, but even they can't begin to capture the staggering thrust served up by the 918 when you floor the throttle, its nose hoovering in the horizon at an unseemly rate of knots. With the petrol and electric motors working in tandem, there's a never-ending stream of immense, instant power, from any revs at any speed.

Hypercars pumping out nearly 900bhp are traditionally a little … challenging to drive. Not the 918. With four-wheel drive, four-wheel steer and torque vectoring, it helps you keep all that power going in the right direction. The steering is sharp and progressive, and the balance neutral, the 918 telegraphing its ridiculously high limits clear and early. Yes, if you turn off all the electronic assistance and boot it in the wet, it'll wag its tail, but this isn't a hypercar that wants to do sideways silliness. It wants to go improbably fast, be it in a straight line or around a track.

If you want, of course, the 918 can play green. Hit the 'E' button and you have a four-wheel-drive electric supercar, one capable of going 20-odd miles on battery power alone and outpacing hot hatches without going anywhere near the V8. In combined mode, it officially does 94mpg and returns just 70g/km of CO_2. Which would make it a great way to save cash … if a new 918 didn't cost over £700,000.

But who's worried about zero emissions when you've got a race-spec V8 to play with? Especially one that sounds as good as the 918's. At low revs, the sound is dominated by the whine of the electric motors, but by 3000rpm or so, the flat-crank V8 starts to dominate proceedings, with its hard and guttural growl that climbs to a furious howl at the engine's 9250rpm top end, a noise that sets every atom in your body tingling with petrolhead pleasure.

Maybe the 918's greatest achievement is that it's a hypercar you could realistically use daily, should the desire so take you. The visibility is good and the driving position comfortable. Porsche boasts that the windscreen wipers function perfectly at 214mph (how many other companies would even test that?). The bespoke navigation is stunning, operated through a touchscreen that recognizes smartphone-style 'swipe' gestures.

Some might complain that the 918 would have been a purer hypercar with the V8 alone and no electric gubbins. But Porsche says a petrol-only 918 would have posted a far slower Nurburgring lap time than the hybrid's searing 6m57s effort. Green technology officially hijacked.

VOLKSWAGEN

XL1

TWO HUNDRED AND SIXTY-ONE MILES PER GALLON. That's the official economy figure of the VW XL1, the most efficient car ever created. And that mpg reading isn't some number plucked from the world of concept: the XL1 is a real, functioning production car, available to buy for normal humans (though admittedly in very limited numbers and for quite a lot of money).

How does it achieve such Scrooge-like economy? Because, though it might not look like one, the XL1 is a supercar. Only the 'super' in this case refers to being frugal, not going fast. It's VW's most advanced car ever, with a carbon fibre tub and carbon fibre panels – just like the McLaren P1, no less – and using every trick in the book to cut through the air as cleanly as possible, even ditching side mirrors in favour of tiny bullet cameras. The XL1's drag coefficient is 0.19, making it slipperier through the air than a bullet.

OK, the little VW isn't exactly quick. The XL1 packs a tiny two-cylinder diesel and an electric motor that produce a combined 75bhp, and can run independently or together. It takes 12.7 seconds to get to 62mph, so you won't be giving any Golf GTis a run for their money. But in a car that weighs just 795kg, that's enough shove to see the XL1 keeping pace with motorway traffic.

And burn virtually no fuel while doing so. So slippery is the XL1 that, at 60mph, it requires just 8bhp to maintain a steady speed. It's so parsimonious that, were you to achieve the official economy figure on a drive from London to Land's End, you'd spend less than a fiver on fuel.

ITALY

Soul. Passion. Yep, that's two quid into James May's patented *Top Gear* Italian Car Road Test Cliché Swear Box right there. As ever, Captain Slow was annoyingly correct, because – cliché though it may be to point it out – Italian cars possess a spirit no other country can match. True, they may occasionally fall catastrophically to pieces, and true, their sat navs may occasionally decide to redirect you to Burkina Faso when all you really wanted to do was find the nearest Sainsbury's. But when it comes to building conversation-stoppingly beautiful cars that'll stir the deepest reaches of your soul - sorry, your seat-of-feelings-and -sentiments, no-one can top the Italians. Prepare your pound coins and read on.

FOR MOST MILLIONAIRES, OWNING A FERRARI ENZO WOULD BE ENOUGH. Then again, most millionaires aren't James Glickenhaus. So when the American car collector – a man who made his fortune through writing and producing movies, and then on the stock market – fancied a new hypercar to complement his stock of old Ferraris, he commissioned Italian design house Pininfarina to come up with this entirely unique slice of retro wonder.

It's called the P4/5 – a name referencing the legendary Ferrari P3/4 endurance racer of 1967, not the form indicating you've been fired – and it's a glorious blend of past and present.

The chassis underneath is the last-ever brand-new Enzo – a pleasantly high starting point, with a 660bhp, 6.0 litre V12, 217mph top speed and 0–60mph time of 3.3 seconds. But atop those entirely sufficient underpinnings, Pininfarina crafted a body that references Ferrari's greatest Le Mans racers of the late sixties, with a dash of fighter plane thrown in for good measure.

This is no glue-on-aftermarket-spoiler job. The P4/5

boasts over 200 unique parts built to beyond-aerospace standard, from the laser-cut headlight clusters, to the glass, to the butterfly doors and their wonderful milled aluminium hinges, to the carbon fibre body panels, down to the wheels, machined from aluminium.

The result is a car not only stunning, but functional too. The P4/5 develops even more downforce than the Enzo, while making less aero drag, and is 165kg lighter. Point is, this is no concept car. This is a Ferrari, a machine designed to be driven. It came with a ten-year warranty, and, though we don't know exactly how fast it'll go, Glickenhaus confirmed that he'd tested it past 170mph. Museum piece? Forget it.

The P4/5's designer, Pininfarina's Jason Castriota, described it as having 'a jet fighter aesthetic'. 'When people first see it,' said Castriota, 'they have a moment of confusion, because it's challenging to look at. But we wanted to create a piece of art, something timeless, something that you appreciate more the longer you look at it.'

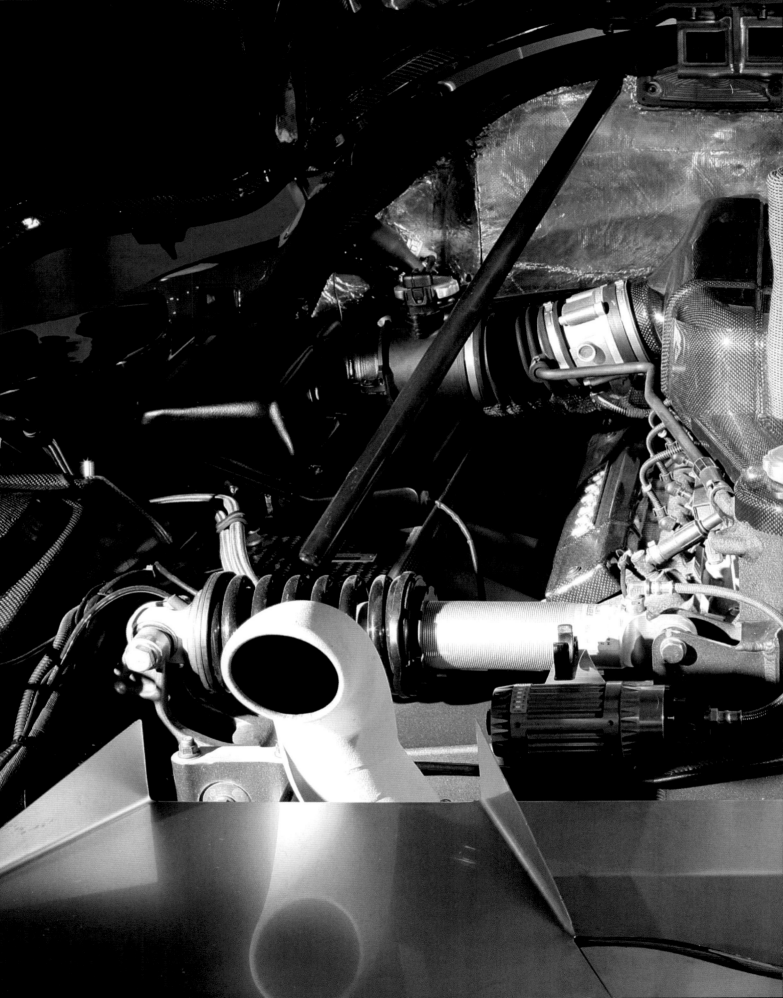

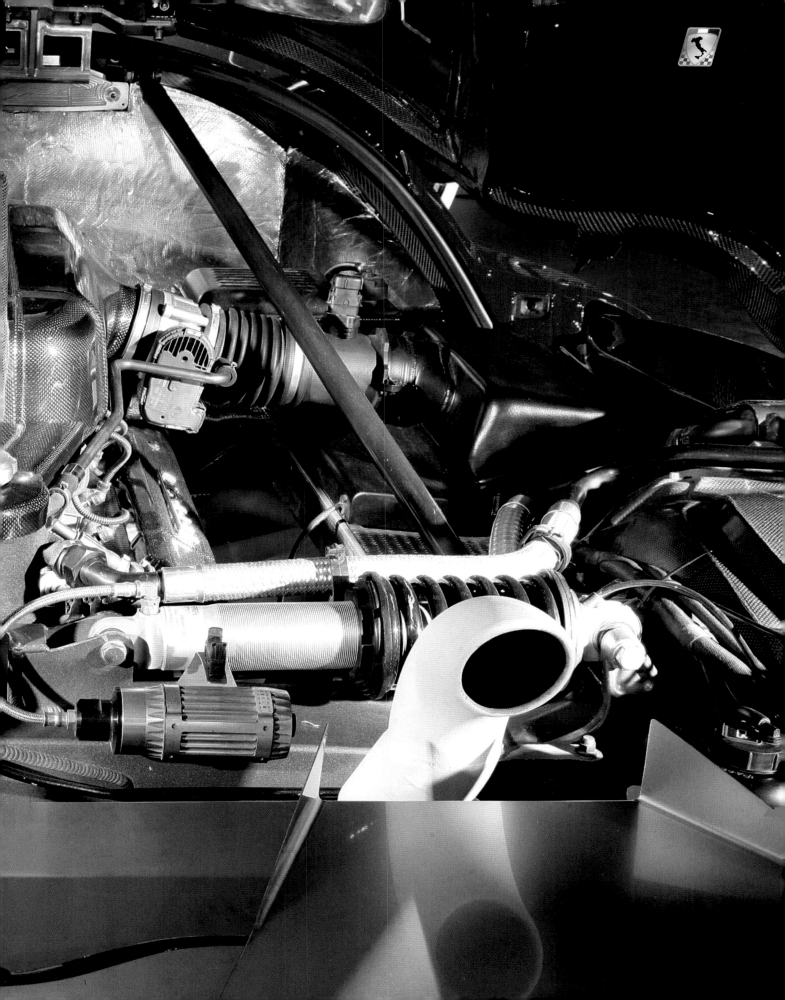

FIAT

500

THE 'NUOVA' FIAT 500 OF 2007 HAD SOME VERY BIG SHOES TO FILL. Actually, that's not quite true. It had some very small, but very significant, shoes to fill. The original 500 of 1957 remains perhaps the ultimate Italian icon: the car that embodies that nation's effortless style; the car that epitomizes Italy's ability to generate miracles from simple ingredients; the car that mobilized an entire generation. And, perhaps more importantly, the car in which that generation learned how to do the *amore* thing in a layby at twilight.

So – especially considering the fraught difficulty of reinventing a retro icon – it's a mighty achievement that the modern 500 succeeds in capturing La Dolce Vita vibe of its predecessor. Cheap it may be, but the little Fiat neatly sidesteps needless parsimony, turning its humble Panda underpinnings into something simple yet evocative.

Since the new 500's introduction, Fiat has gone about churning out hotter and yet hotter versions, along with cabrios and even a mini-MPV. Perhaps these stretch the halo glow of the original 500 a little too far, for the finest of the modern variants is the simple, straightforward 500 hatch packed with Fiat's delicious 875cc two-cylinder engine.

If you like engineering and you like old motors, you can't help but adore the 500's bubbly two-cylinder. Even at idle, it emits a cheery array of splutters and pops, climbing to a chuntering buzz as you rise through the revs. It sounds wonderful – albeit a mite intrusive if you don't appreciate the noise of a small scooter with a hole in its exhaust – and produces a surprising amount of shove.

No, the 500 doesn't handle with the crisp precision of, say, the new Mini, instead bumbling down the road with a double helping of bounce and tilt. But that's all part of the charm, for there's an ineffable zing about the new 500. It puts a smile on your face. Just like the original.

LAMBORGHINI
ESTOQUE

IF LAMBORGHINI WAS TO RELEASE A FOUR-DOOR, FOUR-SEAT SUPER-SALOON RIVAL TO ASTON MARTIN'S RAPIDE and the Porsche Panamera, how would such a car look? 2008's Estoque concept – named, of course, after the sword that a matador plunges between a bull's eyes to finish the brute off once and for all – gave the world a tantalizing glimpse of what might happen if Italy's maddest manufacturer departed from its traditional diet of mid-engined supercars and diversified into the world of front-engine limo-things.

Quite a large glimpse, as it goes. The Estoque measures over five metres long and two metres wide, but stands just 135cm tall, giving it an almost impossibly broad, squat stance and making it very tricky to squeeze into a supermarket parking space.

Lamborghini has done four-door cars before – successfully with the super-cool Espada, rather less successfully with the 'Rambo Lambo' LM002, the gruesome off-roader much beloved by Colonel Gaddafi – but the Estoque (pronounced Es-tock-eh) carries an if-Batman-did-airport-transfers vibe all of its own.

And, being a Lambo, it was officially Not Slow. The concept packed the 5.2-litre V10 from the Gallardo, but – said Lamborghini – could easily have fitted the firm's monstrous V12, or even a hybrid powertrain. This was no pie-in-the-sky design concept, but a car that was, in Lambo's own words, '100 per cent production feasible'.

'It's ready to go,' said then Lamborghini design director Manfred Fitzgerald when the Estoque was unveiled. 'This car represents a major statement of intent. The Estoque meets all necessary legislation. We are absolutely serious about this car.'

Absolutely serious Lamborghini may have been, but more than half a decade later we're still waiting for the production Estoque to arrive. A pity: as the rest of the world's 'luxury brands' expand their portfolios with big-selling but depressingly predictable SUVs, a Lamborghini super-saloon would have stood out from the millionaire crowds.

430 SCUDERIA

JUST CALL IT SCUD. A SHORT, FAST NAME FOR A SHORT, FAST CAR, A CAR THAT PROPELLED THE FERRARI 430 INTO A WHOLE NEW REALM OF TRACK-HONED EVIL. At £172,500, it was some £28,000 more expensive than the standard car. And for this premium, Ferrari gave you … less. No radio, no carpets, no soundproofing, welds that appeared to have been done by apes, and carbon fibre where you'd expect to find something more substantial.

Modified pistons and a revised exhaust system added an extra 20bhp to the 430's 4.3-litre V8, boosting power to 503bhp. It weighs a full 100kg less than the standard car. In numerical terms, the results were incontrovertible: 0–62mph took 3.5 seconds, top speed stood at 198mph.

But numbers aren't everything. Too often, when manufacturers attempt to do the lightweight, track-honed thing, you end up with a car that, though faster, is more uncomfortable, more expensive and exactly no better than the car on which it was based. But not the Scud. All Ferrari's fettling resulted in a car that drove like a Ferrari, with all the passion of a Ferrari: a 430, only more so. It felt raw, crude and dirty, serving up a wall of power and sound, all the way up to 8700rpm.

That's what the Scud was really all about: unbelievable, staggering, joyous noise. That was the one sensation you experienced beyond all others: the volume, the din. The headache. You were dimly aware of some speed, and some surprisingly compliant suspension. You vaguely registered how smoothly the speed changed. And then you had to go and have another Nurofen.

Its four-point harnesses and extra stability control settings no doubt tagged the Scud as a car aimed at ghastly track-day enthusiasts whose wives hate them. But it wasn't. It was a car for the road, a car for anywhere. The car the 430 always wanted to be.

ALFA ROMEO

8C SPIDER

IN 2007, ALFA ROMEO UNVEILED THE JAW-DROPPING 8C COUPÉ. IT WAS, QUITE SIMPLY, THE MOST BEAUTIFUL CAR OF THE MODERN ERA, a beguiling blend of long nose, short tail and stunning lines.

Problem was, it wasn't much cop to drive. 'The suspension feels like it's made from old teabags!' complained Clarkson when he tested the 8C around the *Top Gear* track.

So a few eyebrows were raised when, a year later, Alfa announced it was to chop the top off its V8 masterpiece to create the 8C Spider. See, the general rule is that turning a coupé into a convertible is pretty much guaranteed to worsen the handling: getting rid of all that sturdy metal atop the driver's head doesn't do much for a car's structural stability.

But somehow, in the 8C Spider, Alfa created a car that was not only as beautiful and even better sounding than the coupé, but better to drive, too. The Alfa engineers revised the Spider's entire suspension set-up, making it more predictable, less wooden. While you never knew quite when the Coupé might bite, the Spider is more confidence-inspiring, letting you use more of its grip to have more fun.

It's safe to say that replacing the hard top with soft did nothing to harm the two-seater's stunning looks. You still get reams of beautiful carbon fibre and leather in the cabin, and, with the 450bhp Maserati-derived 4.7-litre V8 left unaltered, it still goes like a scalded bull, getting past 62mph in 4.5 seconds, and running past 180mph.

And what noise. Without a roof in the way, you're able to appreciate, in full surround sound, the extraordinary, brutal opera of that huge V8 and stack of tailpipes. It makes a deep-chested, animalistic noise, far deeper than a Ferrari V8. You could play heavy-metal tunes on this thing.

If you could afford to buy one, of course. The 8C Spider cost £174,000, with just 500 ever built. A car as rare as it is beautiful.

MURCIÉLAGO
SV SPIDER

DV·556HA BO

THE LAMBORGHINI MURCIÉLAGO LP670-4 SUPER VELOCE. A VERY LONG TITLE FOR A CAR WITH A VERY SIMPLE PURPOSE: to send the Murciélago out with a bang. After eight years in production, and with a new V12 supercar on the way in the shape of the Aventador, Lambo decided to say goodbye to its brutish Murciélago in style. It did so by cooking up what was, at the time, its fastest road car to date, a bewinged, four-wheel-drive beast capable of hauling from nought to 60mph in 3.2 seconds and running all the way to 212mph.

The SV also marked the end of the road for Lamborghini's venerable 'Bizzarrini' V12 engine: the same basic engine that, astonishingly, had served in every one of Lamborghini's 12-cylinder cars since 1963. The Aventador would see an all-new powerplant, but the SV gave the venerable Biz a fitting send-off. This engine, which started life making around 270bhp in the very first Lamborghini, the 350GT, now pumped out a vast 661bhp.

But there was more to the SV than a load of power and a gigantic rear wing. It was also some 100kg lighter than the standard Murciélago, thanks to a new flyweight exhaust and lashings of carbon fibre. The weight loss transformed the SV into a quite different car from the standard Murc, one light and nimble on its feet. 'The results are … astonishing!' beamed Hammond when he tested the SV in Abu Dhabi, racing it on a closed highway against the equally monstrous Mercedes SLR McLaren 722.

The Lambo kept pace with the McMerc all the way, and made an even better noise. In its promotional bumf, Lamborghini proudly boasts the SV emits a range of noises from 'the trumpeting of mighty elephants to the roar of a raging lion'. With any other manufacturer – with any other car – this could be dismissed as hyperbole. But in this case it's true. The SV sounds utterly astonishing. In pursuit of weight-saving, the Lambo engineers even chucked away the Murciélago's radio, but that's no hardship here: what would you rather listen to than the glorious noise of that huge V12?

FERRARI
458

OVER THE YEARS, FERRARI HAS BUILT VERY MANY GOOD CARS, AND A FAIR NUMBER OF TRULY EPOCHAL ONES. But every now and again, the Scuderia releases something that moves the supercar world on, not by a generation or two, but by a millennium or two. The 458 is such a car. The mid-engined successor to the 430 (no slouch itself) is arguably the finest-driving Ferrari road car of all time, and thus, by extension, a strong contender for the finest-driving supercar of all time.

Some numbers. The '458' name refers to the car's 4.5-litre V8 – unadorned by turbocharger or hybrid nonsense – that hits the headlines by serving the rear wheels with 562 horsepowers at a cortex-melting, mellifluous 9000rpm. While your ears are being bathed in happy V8 noise, and the hairs on the back of your neck are crackling in delight, the 458 will see its way to 62mph in 3.4 seconds and a top speed just over 200mph. Such speed is kept in check by much F1-inspired aerodynamic trickery. Those black 'whiskers' on the 458's front bumper are rubber-section 'aeroelastic winglets', which deform at high speeds, to cut drag and force more air into the radiators. The underbody is perfectly flat, the 458 producing 140kg of downforce at 120mph.

There's more liberal pilfering of Ferrari's F1 locker on show here. The 458 boasts a race-style steering wheel, with virtually all the important controls – indicators, lights, wipers, starter button, adjustable '*manettino*' – moved onto the front of the wheel. Which is great news when the wheel's pointing straight, but gets a little confusing when you've got half a turn of lock dialled in and all the buttons have shifted 180 degrees from where you left them.

And that's about the only criticism that can be levelled at the glorious 458. This is a sublime, near-telepathic thing to drive fast, one that becomes an almost unsettling extension of your own nervous system as it traces the perfect line through corners, every control fizzing with feedback. The greatest ever? It just might be.

MASERATI

GRANCABRIO

IT TAKES A FULL 28 SECONDS FOR THE GRANCABRIO TO RAISE OR LOWER ITS ROOF, longer than just about any other convertible on the market. This is no criticism. In the GranCabrio's case, such tardiness is a good thing, as it gives any bystanders a little longer to drink in its glorious styling.

Just look at the way the nose resolves into the front wing, the neat downward arc over the rear arch, the upswept kink of the bootlid. That it pulls off the big cabrio act with quite such aplomb is all the more impressive when you consider Maserati never designed the original hard-top GranCoupé to be turned into a convertible.

As bodge-jobs go, then, this isn't a bad one. In fact, the GranCabrio – Italian for 'GrandmotherConvertible', of course – is surely the most stunning four-seat convertible of the century so far. On the face of it, the GC appears to be a straight-up rival for straight-laced German produce like the BMW M6. But while not even the most dyed-in-the-wool devotee of all things Teutonic has ever looked at a BMW M6 and thought, 'I must immediately mortgage a vital organ to possess this', the GranCabrio is so beautiful that even a brief glance will have you quietly contemplating whether you could get by with just one lung.

And that's before starting it up. With a naturally aspirated V8, the GranCabrio emits a full-blooded war cry that builds to a soprano scream above 3000rpm. But despite that high-revving V8 up front, the GranCabrio isn't a straining-at-the-leash sports car. Which isn't to say it's bad at tackling a good road. It isn't. With that great expanse of fabric – or, with the roof down, great expanse of nothing – you might expect the GranCabrio to shimmy and shake in the corners, but it steers well and stops immaculately, while its even weight distribution means the GC is never less than balanced.

But weighing in at very nearly two tonnes – before you add driver and three gorgeous passengers – the big Maser doesn't like to be driven hard. It prefers to ooze along: cultured, confident, refined. It's about sensation, noise and atmosphere. And a very slow roof.

PAGANI
ZONDA R

OVER THE YEARS, MANY MANUFACTURERS HAVE ATTEMPTED TO BREAK INTO FERRARI AND LAMBORGHINI'S EXTRAVAGANT SUPERCAR CLUB. But only Pagani has managed to pick the lock with its sofa-chewing Zonda. Introduced in 1999, this mid-engined V12 masterpiece grew from a 390bhp supercar to, by the end of its life, an Enzo-rivalling hyper-thing making nearly 700bhp.

So how to give the Zonda an appropriate send-off before the introduction of Pagani's all-new Huayra? With the deranged Zonda R: the most brilliant, yet useless, car of the twenty-first century.

Useless? Unquestionably so. Why? Because the Zonda R is a race car, and thus entirely illegal to drive on the public road. But it doesn't conform to a single piece of racing legislation, so you can't enter it into any recognized race series on the planet.

And you can't even turn up at your local track day to give it a thrash. The Zonda R is so blaringly loud that it will fail the noise restrictions of any UK circuit, meaning you'll have to build your own race-track in the middle of some wilderness. The going rate for one of those nowadays is around six billion quid. Factor in the £1.5m to buy a Zonda R and you can see this car represents a very expensive hobby indeed.

Useless it may be, but at least the Zonda R is sublimely useless. It ditched the 7.3-litre AMG V12 engine in favour of a 6.0-litre AMG racing unit, and was the first Zonda to be sold with a flappy-paddle racing gearbox. It weighed the same as a Ford Fiesta and packed 740bhp. It went like nothing on earth, screaming like a psychopath in a gin trap and hurling itself at the end of a runway with utter savagery. And, with a giant new set of carbon ceramic brakes, the R stops as brutally as it accelerates, braking from 125mph to a dead stop in just 4.3 seconds. 'The only way to stop faster,' noted Jeremy when he tested it in 2011, 'is to hit a tree.'

LAMBORGHINI

SESTO ELEMENTO

SESTO ELEMENTO. ITALIAN FOR 'SIXTH ELEMENT'.

Which, on the period table, is carbon. This is no coincidence. The Sesto Elemento – essentially a very special edition Gallardo – is a love letter to the black stuff.

True, many supercars feature a smattering of carbon fibre: perhaps a bit across the dash, or even a rear wing rendered in the black weave. The Sesto Elemento takes its obsession rather further. This thing is made of almost nothing but carbon fibre.

The Lambo's propshaft, suspension and even its wheel rims are forged from carbon. Its body is a revolutionary blend of carbon and plastic, jointly developed by Lamborghini and Boeing.

Lamborghini's dedication to weight-saving didn't stop with liberal use of the sixth element. So desperate were the Sant'Agata engineers to pare back the Sesto Elemento to its very minimum that they refused even to paint it: the body's colour comes from flecks of crystal embedded in the carbon-plastic. And you don't get seats, instead perching upon a few sparse pads stuck directly to the chassis.

Which means the Sesto Elemento doesn't weigh very much. A little under a tonne, in fact, which – given it's packing a 570bhp edition of the 5.2-litre V10 engine from the Gallardo – is faintly astonishing.

The large power number and very small weight number combine to make a car that's superbike fast. The Sesto Elemento will get from nought to 62mph in a scant 2.5 seconds, which is as fast as a Veyron. As fast as anything. It'll do 217mph flat-out, at which point your ears will be bleeding copiously.

But shearing every unnecessary gram from a car doesn't just give it a devastating set of vital statistics. It also makes it impossibly agile. The Sesto Elemento turns like a swallow, and lets you brake later for corners than you ever thought possible. It's a car imbued with almost telepathic qualities.

'People talk about being at one with a car,' grinned Hammond when he thrashed the Sesto Elemento around Italy's Imola circuit. 'I've grown a car out of my hands and feet!'

NEW
STRATOS

THE LANCIA STRATOS IS PERHAPS THE MOST ICONIC RALLY CAR OF ALL TIME. First shown in 1971, the mid-engined, wedge-shaped Stratos won three WRC titles on the trot between 1974 and 1976, cementing its reputation as one of the greatest Italian sports cars of all time.

But once the Stratos died in the late seventies, Lancia never revived its mid-engined, rear-drive icon. So, some 30 years later, a German millionaire and rally enthusiast named Michael Stoschek took it upon himself to bring the Stratos legend kicking and screaming into the twenty-first century.

He did a proper job of it. Stoschek's team started with a Ferrari 430 Scuderia and then got busy with the heavy-duty machinery. The 430's aluminium panels were tossed out, and its aluminium spaceframe chassis shortened by 20cm and welded to an FIA-approved steel roll cage. The A-pillars were reprofiled to accommodate the wraparound windscreen, the body and interior made pretty much entirely of carbon fibre. Even the door bins were enlarged, designed to hold crash helmets in a cute homage to the original Stratos's most memorable interior feature.

A new ECU and bespoke titanium exhaust system saw power rise from 503bhp to 532bhp, with weight cut by some 150kg. Which meant 0–62mph in 3.3 seconds and somewhere close to 190mph all-out.

The original Stratos was never a car for the faint-hearted. Out on the road, the new one stays entirely true to its heritage. With a shorter wheelbase and slightly higher centre of gravity than the 430 Scud, the idiocy threshold is somewhat lower than in most modern supercars, but drive it in the dry with a decent helping of bravery and you'll discover one of the most entertaining, best-executed cars of the twenty-first century.

A fitting homage to the original Stratos, with just one tiny fly in the ointment: though Stoschek planned to build 40 cars, Ferrari wiped its hands of the project, banning its suppliers from having any part in the new Lancia. It was a move that effectively limited this gorgeous, stubby racer to a single example. Spoilsports.

FERRARI

FF

IF, AT THE TURN OF THE MILLENNIUM, YOU'D PUT A TENNER ON FERRARI BUILDING A FOUR-WHEEL-DRIVE ESTATE CAR, the odds would have been so long that, by now, you'd have made enough money to buy, well, a Ferrari FF. All £230-odd grand of it.

For a four-wheel-drive estate car is precisely what the Ferrari FF is. Of course, being Ferrari, this is hardly a straight-laced rival for, say, an Audi A6 Avant. For a start, the FF is constructed around a screaming 6.3-litre V12 churning out 660bhp, a development of the engine found in the Enzo, a car that's rarely classified as a family runabout. That makes the FF the only estate in the world capable of getting from nought to 62mph in 3.7 seconds and on to a top speed of 208mph.

Even so, this is very much a practical family car. The FF provides ample seating for four, its boot about the same size as that of a Ford Focus. Though, with a huge exhaust system lurking below its floor,

anything you put in the back is liable to get lightly toasted – and, when you get hard on the throttle and detonate all 660 of those horses onto the tarmac, lightly obliterated too. If you've ever wondered how your entire weekly shop might taste when blended into a giant, pulpy smoothie, the FF provides a quick answer.

Clearly deciding an estate Ferrari wasn't unusual enough, Maranello decided to treat its biggest car to four-wheel drive as well, albeit in predictably unconventional form.

The FF retains rear-wheel drive in normal driving, a second gearbox shoving power to the front wheels only when things get slippy. Which makes this the first Ferrari in which you might safely tackle a snowy road: good news if you need to get to your luxury mountaintop chalet in the Swiss Alps.

Amongst its many oddities, perhaps the FF's oddest oddity is its name. FF, says Ferrari, is short for 'Ferrari Four'. Which makes this the, um, Ferrari Ferrari Four. Boutros Boutros-Ghali would surely approve.

LAMBORGHINI
GALLARDO STS

A MASSIVE REAR WING. IT'S A CHILDISH BUT EXTREMELY EFFECTIVE WAY OF RAISING A CAR'S RANKING IN THE GREAT SCALE OF ALL THINGS DESIRABLE. And wings don't come much bigger than the ironing board propped upon the back of the Gallardo Super Trofeo Stradale. It's a fittingly extreme spoiler for the most extreme road-legal Gallardo, a car that boasts a 563bhp 5.2-litre V10 feeding all four wheels, a 0–62mph time of 3.4 seconds and a top speed of 199mph.

This isn't a car for the faint of heart. The STS gets four-point race harnesses and a full roll cage, and weighs 70kg less than the standard car thanks to a quick-release carbon rear deck. It requires a steely nerve to drive. Yes, the Gallardo STS is four-wheel drive, but the system is biased to throw most of its power to the rear tyres. Combine that with a mid-engined layout that slugs more of the car's weight over the rear wheels than the fronts, and you're looking at a car that'll do lurid great slides if the road is wet or icy.

In the second decade of the twenty-first century, there's no denying the Gallardo STS is feeling a little long in the tooth. The ride is a mite fidgety against the astonishing poise of the Ferrari 458 and McLaren 12C. There's no radio and the interior is bare carbon, so the only soundtrack on the move is a brain-blending combination of vibration and V10.

But the STS redeems all its flaws with that vast rear wing, nicked wholesale from the 'Super Trofeo' cars that run in Lamborghini's one-make race series, a rear wing which sits so high on its twin posts that it's invisible from the driver's seat. It's a spoiler that serves a function beyond impressing every ten-year-old boy in a 50-mile radius. The extra downforce it provides helps the STS feel astonishingly stable at speed, as if nailed to the road with metal bolts. This is a car that feels safer at 170mph than at 70mph. Legal limits permitting, of course …

HUAYRA

HOW DO YOU FOLLOW A CAR LIKE THE ZONDA?

As impressive first acts go, the car that propelled Pagani from obscurity into the top tier of the global supercar fraternity in a single leap is about as impressive as they come.

When the time came to replace its ageing, gorgeous Zonda – as it bowed out with the certifiable 'R' edition – Pagani, being Pagani, decided not to make a cheaper, less extravagant supercar: one more accessible to the masses; one that might sell hundreds, rather than tens, each year. No, Pagani decided the only way to follow the maddest supercar in history was to go … even madder.

So, to create the Huayra – pronounced 'Why-Rah' – design genius Horatio Pagani started with a blank sheet of paper: there's barely a part carried over from the old car. Out went the Zonda's 7.3-litre naturally aspirated V12, replaced by a new twin-turbo V12 – again sourced from Mercedes's evil AMG division – making a certifiable 730bhp and 738lb·ft of torque. In a car that weighs just 1350kg, that's about the same power-to-weight ratio as a Veyron SuperSport. But the Veyron has four-wheel drive. The Huayra puts its power through the rear wheels alone. This is not a car to be messed with.

Unlike the high-revving Zonda, the Huayra makes its power like a monstrous diesel engine, doing all its best work below 5500rpm. It doesn't sound like a traditional Italian supercar either: no high-revving choral warble, rather a strange, addictive mix of white-noise induction and space-age whine. Imagine a Group B rally car on full-throttle lift mixed with the air-splitting roar of a Space Shuttle launch and you're getting somewhere close: a low-frequency salvo that batters you in the chest and leaves a dull ache in your lungs. It's extraordinary.

As is the rest of the car. The Huayra's central cell is formed of Pagani's favourite material, a super-strong blend of carbon fibre and titanium dubbed 'carbotanium'. This is officially the coolest name for any material in the history of ever. Company chief Horatio Pagani insisted the wing mirrors must look like the eyes of a beautiful woman. They actually do. This is lightly disturbing.

The Huayra isn't pretty in the classical sense, but it's an intriguing, impressively functional piece of design. The passenger doors are up-hinging gullwings like those on a Mercedes SLS, though even more bizarre. They're not only deliciously extravagant, but also make the Huayra far easier to get in and out of than the Zonda, a car that required the flexibility of a malnourished Chinese gymnast to enter or exit gracefully.

The Pagani's interior is an extraordinary mish-mash of past and future. Every rocker switch and button is exquisitely milled from aluminium, sat atop bare carbon and aluminium studded with LED lights that shine through clear crystal. And, just as a finishing touch, the cabin is overlaid with defiantly old-school buckles and leather straps. It shouldn't work, but somehow it does.

As does the Huayra's cleverest trick, a set of aerodynamic flaps – two at the front, two at the rear – which pop up and down independently to keep the car stable, controlled by a very clever computer reacting to throttle and brake position, along with all sorts of sensors plastered over the car. So in a fast left-hand corner, for example, the Huayra's front left-hand flap will pop up to keep the car's nose flat and counter the weight shift to the outside of the curve. Under hard braking, the rear paddles will open to stop the car from standing on its nose.

Such aero trickery helps contribute to a car that's not only incandescently fast – nought to 62mph in 3.2 seconds, a top speed around 230mph – but more deliciously bonkers than anything else on the planet. A Veyron might be marginally faster, a McLaren P1 marginally more precise, but nothing makes a statement like the Huayra. Zonda successfully succeeded.

PAGANI HUA

FERRARI

F12

FOR ALL FERRARI'S ACCLAIMED DALLYING IN MID-ENGINED SPORTS CARS LIKE THE 458 and hyper-things like the Enzo and LaFerrari, front-engined V12 supercars remain Maranello's heartland. So when Ferrari does a new front-engined V12 supercar, you can safely assume it's going to be a bit special.

And the F12 isn't just a bit special. It's special to the power of several. The replacement for the iconic 599 stood, at its launch, as Ferrari's fastest ever road car, capable of getting from nought to 62mph in 3.1 seconds and past 124mph barely five seconds later. It won't stop running until 211mph. That makes it faster than the Enzo, and not just in a straight line either: until the release of the LaFerrari, nothing with a Prancing Horse badge and licence plate had gone around the firm's Fiorano test track quicker than the F12.

The 6.3-litre V12 tucked behind those front wheels is a veritable symphony of engineering. Driving the rear wheels through a genius double-clutch gearbox that delivers all-but-instantaneous changes, it makes 730bhp and a walloping 509lb·ft of torque, and has more power, everywhere, than you could ever need. Nail the throttle at any engine speed over 2000rpm and within 0.7 seconds – the blink of any eye – you'll have 90 per cent of maximum acceleration. What 90 per cent of the F12's maximum acceleration means, in non-maths terms, is this: shocking, savage fastness.

Shocking even to a grizzled old pro like Clarkson, who, despite praising it as 'light, nimble, sharp and spectacular', discovered the F12 to be something of a slippery customer when he tested it in Scotland. Sorry, Hertfordshire. 'While the car is fine, I am struggling,' admitted JC. 'It is a bit … frantic in here. It feels like you're sort of out of control. You put your foot down and you think, "Oh yes", and then immediately you think, "Oh no, actually". Too scary.

'You can't even sneeze when you drive this car, because if you did … well, they'd have to hose you off the road.'

ALFA ROMEO
4C

TOP GEAR HAS LONG MAINTAINED THAT YOU CAN'T BE A TRUE PETROLHEAD UNTIL YOU OWN AN ALFA, but, excluding the very expensive, very-limited-edition 8C, the first decade of the twenty-first century served up very little in the way of Alfa Romeos you'd really want to own. Sure, the Brera and Spider were both devastatingly pretty, but, truth be told, neither was especially good to drive. Or own, if you liked your electronics of the 'working' variety. The Mito? The Giulietta? Both entirely serviceable, but entirely serviceable rivals to the Ford Focuses and Volkswagen Polos of this world rather than pulse-quickening sports-things. Slim pickings indeed for the Alfa virgin wishing to be indoctrinated into the Official World of Petrolhead.

Until, that is, the 4C concept was unveiled. It sounded like the Alfa the world had wanted for decades: very light, very fast, and jaw-snappingly beautiful. It was to be the first car in its price bracket outside the rarefied world of supercars to get a carbon fibre tub,

making it phenomenally lightweight – just 895kg without liquids or driver on board. Such a Gillian McKeith attitude to weight saving meant the 4C could make the most of every one of its 237 horsepowers, generated by a 1.8-litre turbocharged four-cylinder. In fact, so much was the 4C said to make of its modest power that it would get from nought to 62mph in a sparse 4.5 seconds – true supercar performance without the downsides of supercar economy. Or a supercar price tag: initial projections had the 4C costing barely more than a high-end hot hatch.

And then, before the 4C concept became production, things started to get a little wobbly. We discovered that, instead of a simple, straightforward manual gearbox, the 4C would instead employ a flappy-paddle, dual-clutch effort. The elegant headlights of the concept were switched for a set of clusters resembling the surface of a moon after a botched NASA landing. The price, too, rose from low-spec Nissan 370Z money to top-

spec Porsche Cayman money: a dangerous place to be.

So how did the 4C turn out? The Alfa we've all been waiting for, or an expensive mis-hit? A little of both, in truth. Faced with an empty, winding Alpine pass, you'd plump for the former. With its unassisted steering – no fingertip-light power-assisted set-up here – the 4C is simply sensational to thread down a twisty road, turning in sharply, goading you to brake far deeper than you'd ever dare in a full-weight car. Good thing, then, that its Brembo brakes are magnificent. There's masses of grip, while the chassis is balanced, stable and neutral. And it feels quick, hurling itself down the road with fine, fizzing enthusiasm. The 4C's shape, too, is surely everything the world wants from an Alfa coupé: short, squat, virtually wider than it is long.

However (because with Alfa there's always a however), it's a long way from perfect. On less-than-marble-smooth roads, the Alfa hops around like a cat on a hotplate: sniffing out every camber and bump, tugging at its steering and weaving between lanes. Get hard on the brakes into a wonky section of tarmac, and you might just end up a lane or two away from where you expected to be. It's not a quiet companion either, road- and wind-noise merrily beating their way into the 4C's bare cabin.

There's more waywardness. That flappy-paddle gearbox forms a frustrating barrier of technology between squishy driver and oily engine, refusing to shift gear with quite the snappiness it should. Alfa claims the 4C's 'box is faster at certain increments than that of the Ferrari 458. *Top Gear* respectfully disputes this.

So it's far from perfect, the 4C, but what Alfa ever was? If you want to spend £45,000 on a polished sports car, buy a Porsche Cayman. But if you want a car brimming with Italian character, a car that does things its own way for better or worse, a car for petrolheads prepared to endure a little pain to look this good, the 4C is the authentic article.

MASERATI
QUATTROPORTE

QUATTROPORTE. A FINE NAME, ONE BRIMMING WITH ITALIAN PASSION AND THE PROMISE OF MANY CYLINDERS AND MUCH FASTNESS. The truth, of course, as anyone with a rudimentary grasp of Italian will tell you, is far more prosaic: '*Quattroporte*' is simply Italian for 'four-door'.

And the Quattroporte is a four-door that makes no pretence of being a small car. The latest version measures a full 526cm from nose to bootlid, and manages to make even 21-inch wheels look modest within its vast frame. That said, the QP is lighter than it once was, thanks to extensive use of aluminium. In the back, there's more legroom than even an NBA squad could use, but the Quattroporte is one of those limos in which you're more likely to find the owner up front behind the wheel.

Despite its bulk, the QP is a car that shrinks about you out on the road: it steers well and hustles from corner to corner with the wieldiness of something far smaller. There's even a 'Sport' button, though this fails to make things any more sporty, only rather more jiggly and uncomfortable.

Not that you'll notice if you spec the 523bhp, twin-turbo V8, which revs to a strident 7200rpm. That'll haul the Quattroporte from nought to 62mph in 4.7 seconds and on to a top speed of 190mph, which is frankly rather faster than a two-tonne limousine should ever need go.

The cabin is lined with much leather and wood, but also a few mistakes. The air vents are plasticky, the steering wheel is butt-ugly and the gear selector is dreadfully fiddly to use. In a German limo, these flaws would be a matter of grave concern. But the Quattroporte somehow manages to turn its foibles into endearing personality traits. No, it doesn't pack the same baffling volume of technology as a Mercedes S-Class, but makes up for it with a rakish swagger that none of the German luxobarges can match. This is a big car with soul. That's at least three quid in the Italian cliché box, isn't it?

LAMBORGHINI
AVENTADOR ROADSTER

THE AVENTADOR ROADSTER ISN'T A CAR. It's a deliriously complex work of industrial art, a triumph of design that makes every other supercar in the world – with the possible exception of Pagani's Zonda and Huayra – look as if they're just not trying enough. It's also the finest portable sound system on sale: the Aventador's 6.5-litre, 691bhp V12 is a hymn to furious, normally aspirated combustion in an era that's hell-bent on adding turbos or hybrid modules. It revs to 8500rpm, and does so in a great maelstrom of 12-cylinder fury.

Which is one very good reason why you'd have the convertible Aventador rather than the coupé: to make the most of that wonderful noise. And you'd also take the Roadster because it's simply more splendid, revelling in its sheer silliness. Less driver-focused? Forget it. Honestly, if you get to the point, out on the road, of noticing any dynamic difference between the Aventador coupé and the roadster, you're approximately point-eight of a second from an enormous crash. The lack of a roof makes you feel less trapped, more in touch with the workings of that giant, glorious engine.

Unfortunately the Aventador Roadster is somewhat slower than the coupé on which it's based. Since this means a 0–62mph time of 3.0 seconds rather than 2.9, we suspect most potential owners will cope. Top speed stands at the same 217mph as the coupé.

It's a simple spider. There's no clever folding-roof mechanism here, rather a pair of carbon fibre roof panels (each weighing just 3kg) that the owner must pop from the roofspace and stow in the Aventador's front boot. Once done, this leaves approximately enough room for a pair of socks.

Or a box of paracetamol. Just a few minutes alone with the Roadster's single-clutch, paddle-shift gearbox will inform you that this isn't a friendly, accessible supercar. Slip the transmission into 'Race' mode and the Aventador delivers gearshifts with a thuggish thump to the back of your head, anneolithic transmission against the digital-era cleverness of the double-clutch boxes in the Ferrari 458 and McLaren 12C. But when it looks this good and sounds, who gives a damn?

ALFA ROMEO
TOURING
DISCO VOLANTE

WHAT SHOULD YOU DO IF YOU'RE THE SORT OF PERSON WHO RATHER FANCIES AN ALFA ROMEO 8C but thinks it, at a piffling hundred-and-something grand, just too cheap and, with a production run of 500 cars, just too common? You head to Milan's Touring Superleggera coachbuilders and ask them to whip you up a Disco Volante, that's what you do. And Touring Superleggera will say, why, of course, please give us an enormous amount of money, and also an Alfa 8C coupé for us to chop into small bits.

Yes, that's right. The only way to create the masterpiece that is the Disco Volante – its name means 'flying saucer' in Italian – is to destroy the masterpiece that is the Alfa 8C, the car widely regarded as the most beautiful of the twenty-first century. But such is the sacrifice you must make for a Disco Volante: to allow Touring's artisans to set their angle grinders to the luscious bodywork of your newly purchased 8C, stripping it back to its chassis and drivetrain before crafting a new aluminium skin around the Alfa's skeleton.

If you're going to dismember the prettiest car of the last 20 years, you'd better build something pretty damn special in its place. Thankfully the Disco Volante is traffic-stoppingly unique. It looks, quite simply, like nothing you've ever seen on the road, doing away with the pared-back, sharp-edged aesthetic of just about every other modern sports car in favour of curvaceous, Coke-bottle lines. Those voluptuous panels aren't created by robot, but by a team of hammer-wielding craftsmen, who hand-beat sheets of aluminium into the Disco Volante's phenomenally complex, other-worldly shapes.

Touring leaves the Alfa 8C's basic mechanicals unchanged, and the driving experience is dominated by that vicious, whipcrack V8. Like the 8C, the Disco serves up the full-fat Italian front-engined supercar experience. And, like the 8C, the Disco Volante isn't without its foibles. The six-speed sequential gearbox remains inescapably clunky, the ride as unforgiving as a Guantanamo Bay interrogator. But so immersive is the Disco Volante experience, so decadently characterful, that such rough edges only serve to heighten the drive. Especially when you wind it out and bathe in the extraordinary deluge of sound from its new go-louder exhaust, which growls and booms and sings with reckless abandon.

But despite plentiful reserves of fastness – Touring quotes 0–62mph in 4.2 seconds and a 182mph top speed – most of the time you don't feel the need to drive the Disco at Maximum Stig. This is a machine in which to waft around, basking in the glances of admiration/envy/bemusement, enjoying the bass-to-soprano range of that V8 and the sheer occasion of the thing. The cabin is predictably opulent, the giant sunroof adding a surprisingly airy dimension to the low cockpit, while Touring's interior upgrades are as bespoke and immaculately executed as anything on the planet. Naturally you may have any shade or texture of trim you might desire, but also, should the dubious urge seize you, the option of your own, literally inimitable leather.

'We have this material, it is many, many different strips of leather woven together manually,' explains Touring boss Piero Mancardi. 'There is only one place in the world where this is done. It is in Europe, and there are twenty-six ladies who come from Vietnam, where this process was born in the seventies. They were so good at doing it because they have very tiny fingers. You can have thousands of different patterns because you put together so many strips of leather. When you have selected your combination, it is yours forever. We put it in our library, and commit to only make this pattern for you. Your own leather.'

Your personal leather, hand-knitted by tiny-fingered Vietnamese ladies? Very Bond villain, no? But such cat-stroking, volcano-dwelling flamboyance is what the Disco Volante is all about. This is an event of a supercar like no other.

FERRARI

LAFERRARI

THE LAFERRARI IS, QUITE SIMPLY, THE FASTEST FERRARI OF ALL TIME. It generates 950bhp from its revolutionary hybrid powertrain, costs just over a million quid a pop, and will get round Ferrari's Fiorano test track five seconds faster than the legendary Enzo.

It also has a very silly name. LaFerrari? That's 'TheFerrari', right? Which makes this the Ferrari TheFerrari, surely? Between this and the Ferrari Ferrari Four [the FF, page 150], someone in the Ferrari christening department needs a stern talking to.

But if any car had the right to play fast and loose with the conventions of language, it's the LaFerrari. Maranello's flagships are always something pretty special – think 1987's carbon fibre F40, 1995's F1-derived F50 and 2002's astonishing Enzo – but the LaFerrari makes all three look like inside-lane trundlers.

To start with, there's a 6.3-litre, 790bhp V12 wedged in the middle, which is never a bad starting place. To this Ferrari adds an electric motor – utilizing its F1 team's 'HY-KERS' tech and

fed by a lithium ion battery – which adds the equivalent of 160bhp. That combined 950bhp is joined by a haymaking 663lb·ft of torque to imbue the LaFerrari with a 0–62mph time under 3.0 seconds and a top speed – well, let's just say a top speed high enough to see you spending the rest of your natural life in a high-security jail, should you be clocked achieving it on the M25.

Unlike the McLaren P1, which can run on electric power alone for a half-dozen miles or so, the Ferrari shuns such greenology: if the car's switched on, so is the big V12. Fine by us. Lower and narrower than the very low, very narrow Enzo, the LaFerrari is constructed around a tub made of no less than four different types of carbon fibre, one of which is used in the nuclear industry to manufacturer the centrifuges for uranium enrichment. That's pretty much as badass as facts get.

Just 499 LaFerraris shall ever be built, and they're all spoken for. Seems the world's billionaire racers can live with the silly name.

USA

America may not have invented the automobile, but it was the rootin', tootin' US of A that transformed the motor car from a toy of the aristocracy into the twentieth century's must-have transport accessory. It has long been held that Henry Ford's famous 'You can have it in any colour so long as it's black' is the ultimate expression of the mass production techniques he pioneered. Truth is, of course, the Ford founder just had a job-lot of black paint to shift. In the wake of the World War I, as Europe struggled to design cars small enough to squeeze into its existing horse-based, medieval infrastructure, America went the other way, constructing an entire nation around the car. From the very earliest days, American manufacturers demonstrated admirable dedication to big V8 engines and brawny horsepower, and rather less dedication to making their cars actually go round corners. Old habits, it seems, die hard...

FORD
GT

THE FORD GT IS SHAMELESSLY, UNIRONICALLY RETRO. Then again, if you had a car in your back catalogue as iconic and traffic-stopping as the original 1962 GT40, wouldn't you want to remind people about it too?

Ah, the GT40. The car built at the behest of Henry Ford II himself, the car built to give Enzo Ferrari and his Le Mans racers a thorough kicking. The car that, after six years of Ferrari dominance, won France's epic 24-hour race four times on the trot from 1966 to 1969. The car that remains, even today, the only all-American racer ever to win at Le Mans. If ever a car deserved honouring, the GT40 is it.

And the modern GT does a fine job of paying homage to its predecessor. The sixties car stood just 40 inches tall – hence the name – and the new version is only 3 inches loftier. Which, even by supercar standards, is very, very low indeed. Squeezed

behind the driver is a 5.4-litre supercharged V8, its whirring belts visible through the rear-view mirror, which sends 550bhp of all-American muscle straight to the rear wheels. Find a bit of tarmac with sufficient grip, and the GT will get from nought to 62mph in around 3.5 seconds before running all the way to 205mph. That top speed, by the way, is electronically limited: e-nanny removed, the Ford GT repeatedly hit 212mph around the high-speed Nardo bowl in southern Italy.

Those are numbers to worry even the finest of European supercars, but, like its grandpappy, the Ford GT serves up a proudly American experience. Its interior isn't a patch on the masterworks of Ferrari or Pagani, and its handling errs on the brawny. For which read 'occasionally psychotic'. Flawed the GT may be, but it's one of the most addictive supercars of the twenty-first century. Clarkson knows. He bought one. And yes, it broke a lot.

SSC

ULTIMATE
AERO TT

IN 2007, THE SHELBY SUPERCARS ULTIMATE AERO TT SMASHED THE VEYRON'S RECORD FOR THE WORLD'S FASTEST PRODUCTION CAR, clocking a ridiculous 256mph on a 12-mile stretch of closed road in the Nevada desert. OK, so three years later Bugatti – with the help of James May – grabbed the record back with its 268mph Veyron SS, but even so, to pinch the most coveted of crowns from arguably the greatest hypercar in history is pretty much as audacious as coups get.

Especially when you consider the Ultimate Aero was developed for a thousandth of the cost of the Volkswagen Group's prized Veyron. This is a hypercar stripped back to its most essential: the SSC doesn't even get antilock brakes or traction control. This lack of a safety net may weigh fairly heavy on your mind as you spear pass 250mph.

Particularly with a 6.3-litre, 1300bhp twin-turbo offering motivation to the rear wheels through a proper six-speed manual gearbox. That's enough shove to give the Ultimate Aero a 0–62mph time around 2.8 seconds, and – on the perfect road at least – a top speed, says SSC, even higher than that recorded 256mph. As high as 273, apparently.

Aesthetically, the Ultimate Aero is firmly of the Nineties School of Hypercar Design: low, wedgy and wide. The bodywork is all carbon fibre, with a special party piece – twin pop-up air brakes that emerge from the top of the rear wings. So how can SSC sell it for half the price of the million-quid-plus-quite-a-bit Veyron?

The interior offers a clue. Slipping into the Ultimate Aero's quilted leather cabin feels like stepping back in time. The steering wheel is offset to the left while the dials are simple analogue affairs: no multifunction touchscreen here.

Well, with no electronic trickery to deal with, what do you need a touchscreen for anyhow? Once you point the SSC's squashed nose at the horizon, bury the throttle and fire into a realm of acceleration that's the preserve of a precious few hypercars, you won't give a damn about an outdated interior …

TESLA
ROADSTER

NOWADAYS IT'S ALMOST DIFFICULT TO IMAGINE THAT, BEFORE THE TESLA ROADSTER GLIDED SILENTLY ONTO THE SCENE IN 2008, THE NOTION OF AN ELECTRIC CAR WAS WIDELY REGARDED AS DEAD IN THE WATER. Or, rather, dead in the petrol. Now almost every major manufacturer is looking at electric tech, and it's more than a little thanks to this battery-powered Californian convertible.

How did the Tesla succeed where so many electric cars had failed before? By doing a very decent impression of a proper sports car, the cunning fiend. Specifically, by doing a very decent impression of a Lotus Elise, upon which the Tesla is based. The chassis and carbon fibre panels are sourced from Hethel, while the Tesla's ride and handling were also fettled by the Lotus boffins. Which means the little Tesla feels very much like an Elise to drive: sharp as a very sharp nail, quick to change direction, nimble as a caffeinated wasp.

But with one fairly crucial difference. Where the Elise gets a simple four-cylinder petrol engine, the Tesla uses an electric motor fed by no fewer than 6831 individual battery cells. On the downside, this drivetrain does weigh a little more than the Elise's conventional engine, but on the upside it delivers a monstrous slug of torque from a literal standstill: electric motors serve up their full twist from exactly zero rpm. Those 295 torques help the Tesla to 62mph in just 4.1 seconds, with a 250-mile range. If you drive it very, very carefully. Which you won't, because this digital-era sports car packs a surge of acceleration that fires you into the distance at Tron-like pace. It is … well, it's shocking.

Especially because all that fastness occurs in near-total silence, making the Tesla both the ultimate stealth supercar and a genuine hazard for unwary pedestrians. Electric cars haven't yet taken over the world, but they're certainly on the way. In no small part, we have Tesla Motors to thank – or blame – for that.

F150
RAPTOR

THE FORD F150 PICK-UP ISN'T A VEHICLE THAT MOST WOULD LOOK AT AND SAY, 'Y'KNOW WHAT THIS TRUCK NEEDS? MORE.' The standard F150, after all, measures over 5.5m from end to end, and will seat five American footballers in comfort, with enough space on the flatbed for a couple of just-shot buffalo.

But America wasn't built by people who look at giant pick-ups and think, 'Yeah, that'll probably do.' America was built by people who look at giant pick-ups and think, 'Yeah, but what if we made it even more off-road?'

Welcome, then, the F150 Raptor: the evil lovechild of a commercial ute and a Baja buggy. The Raptor is wider than the standard F150, with Dakar-spec suspension offering feet of articulation. The differentials and electronic controls are equally toughened-up. This is, quite simply, the most serious off-roader any mainstream manufacturer has ever built. And it ain't built for plodding, donkey-like, up and down sand dunes at walking pace. It's built for racing, for pounding across American badlands at triple-figure speeds, absorbing boulders the size of grizzlies as it goes.

Oh, and jumping. The Raptor is perhaps the car world's finest leaper, capable of launching its 2.7 tonnes of yee-haw heft many metres into the air off any appropriate yump, before returning to earth with the softest of landings. You can even switch between two-wheel drive or four-, depending on whether your penchant is for face-wrenching grip from those vast off-road tyres, or hilariously incongruous sideways. And with the option of a 6.2-litre, 411bhp V8 engine – which is clearly the one you'd have, because if you're pitching for 'way, way too much', you might at least do it properly – that sideways isn't hard to come by. Some might think the Raptor a little too much. But, as Frasier once sagely noted: if less is more, imagine how much more more would be …

CADILLAC
CTS-V

IT'S OFTEN SAID – NOT LEAST BY THOSE UNINFORMED CLOTS AT *TOP GEAR* – THAT AMERICAN CAR MANUFACTURERS DON'T KNOW A WHOLE LOT ABOUT CORNERS. In the case of the CTS-V, however, that's patently untrue. This supercoupé is made of nothing but corners. Some cars go in for Coke-bottle curves and organic contours. Not this one. The CTS-V looks like it was styled with a breadknife, its edges sharp enough to slice unwary pedestrians, its underbite severe enough to give nightmares to even the hardiest dentist.

But under that low, wide, set-square exterior lurks a brawling muscle car from the old school, a bellowing mammoth that'll happily turn its rear tyres to clouds of acrid smoke at the merest provocation, a hairy-chested alternative to the precise performance machines served up by the German behemoths. At the CTS-V's heart resides a 6.2-litre V8 pounding out 556bhp and 561lb·ft of torque. That continent-twisting power isn't produced through any faddish modern technology – hybrid modules, variable valve timing – but instead a very traditional, very American formula: a pushrod engine supplemented with a whacking great supercharger. Which means you don't have to drag the CTS-V to the limiter to find its sweet spot. Peak torque hits the rear wheels exactly in the middle of the fat rev range, allowing you to wallow in the Cadillac's great mudbath of power.

But, as with all American action heroes, the CTS-V has its share of character flaws. Specifically an interior that, though packed with suede and bucket seats and plenty of infotainment toys, is as cheap and plasticky as the toy in a pound-shop Christmas cracker, and an automatic gearbox with the responsiveness of a clinically obese trucker after six pints of Bud. But it's a charming thug, the CTS-V: a bruiser with a big heart. And one that, on its day, can even exit a bend facing in the right direction…

CORVETTE

ZR-1

IT'S INSANELY VULGAR, IT'S ONLY AVAILABLE IN LEFT-HAND DRIVE, its luggage cover looks like a motel shower curtain, it's much too wide, and in the corners it's a complete madman … So spake Jeremy Clarkson of the Corvette ZR-1, the sofa-chewing, no-frills supercar that might just be the maddest thing to emerge from America since George Dubya Bush himself. Such criticism might reasonably lead you to assume that JC wasn't a fan of the brutish Vette. Quite the opposite: he loved it.

And with good reason. See, over its hundred-and-a-bit years in existence, General Motors has built a lot of cars. Many hundreds of millions of cars, in fact. But never has it built one more powerful or faster than the ZR-1: at least, not one that actually existed in road-going form. This coupé, with its modest Corvette underpinnings, makes a galactic 638bhp: more, even, than a Ferrari Enzo.

The ZR-1's 6.2-litre, supercharged V8 (an engine laughably referred to as 'small-block' by GM) is liberally sprinkled with titanium and other exotic metals. Propelling a car weighing just 1500kg, it clocks the 0–62mph sprint in 3.4 seconds, with 100mph rocking up just 3.6 seconds later. Top speed is 205mph. Scrubbing off that speed is left to a simply enormous set of brakes: the ZR1's front discs come from an Enzo, its rears from a Ferrari 599.

But despite all that tech-heavy goodness, and despite employing a phenomenally complicated magnetic suspension system, the ZR1 isn't exactly … precise in the going-round-bends department. In fact, it's an oversteering, tyre-obliterating nutcase, as Jeremy discovered when he tested the ZR-1 against the Audi R8 around the *Top Gear* track.

'Trying to keep up with an Audi R8 is like trying to win the Grand National while riding a lion that's made out of teeth. And jelly,' grimaced Clarkson between powerslides. 'It wobbles about, and if you're not careful, it bites your arm off …'

FORD
FOCUS

HOW MUCH POWER CAN YOU REASONABLY SHOVE THROUGH A CAR'S FRONT WHEELS? AT THE TURN OF THE MILLENNIUM, CONVENTIONAL WISDOM HELD THAT A FRONT-DRIVER WITH MUCH MORE THAN 200BHP OR SO WAS A RECIPE FOR DISASTER. Torque-steering, ditch-seeking disaster. But conventional wisdom clearly didn't sway Ford's judgement when the Blue Oval set out to brew the most ridiculous hot hatch in the history of ever: the Focus RS500.

In fact, this thing isn't so much a hot hatch as a hot-hot-hot hatch. See, first came the standard Focus, which was very nice, but not especially fast. So Ford made the Focus ST, a 225bhp Golf GTI rival that was nice and also fast. But not fast enough for some, so Ford then cooked up the Focus RS, a 300bhp, double-hot hatch that, the world thought, pushed the limits of front-wheel-drive power about as far as they would go without snapping horribly. But there yet was

more to come: a triple-hot, last hurrah for the MkII Focus.

For the RS500, Ford boosted power from the Focus's 2.5-litre five-cylinder engine to an unprecedented 350bhp, courtesy of a revised ECU, new exhaust and beefier fuel pump. To keep all that power flowing smoothly to the road, Ford employed a trick suspension system called RevoKnuckle, which only two people in the universe understood, but which – according to those two people at least – would quell the tendency of power front-wheel-drive cars to buck their steering wheels in protest at the amount of torque they were being forced to endure.

And, for the most part, it worked. The RS500 was far less undrivable than many anticipated: yes, when hard on the power in the wet, the steering wheel would kick like a branded mule, but most of the time the fast Ford simply served up vast helpings of thrust and enough speed to embarrass all but the most committed driver of an Aston Martin. If ever a hot hatch could be legitimately described as a supercar killer, it's this one.

YOU ARE NOT ALONE. You love the look of the old Porsche 911s, but shudder at the thought of their chuntery engines, lack of mod cons and lightly murderous driving dynamics. What you require, oh tough-to-please Porsche enthusiast, are the services of Singer, a Californian outfit that lovingly crafts some of the most stunning retro-modern car creations on the planet.

Here's how it works. Singer takes pre-1994 911 coupés and strips them back to the very bone, before rebuilding them with materials and techniques from the future: materials and techniques from the cutting edge of the aerospace industry.

So those old-school-looking body panels are rendered in carbon fibre, while the body is strengthened and treated to a leather-wrapped roll cage, plus full adjustable suspension all round. Even that traditional 'ducktail' is reborn as a speed-sensitive spoiler that pops up at 60mph.

Oh, but there's more. The alloys are a nod to the 911's classic Fuchs wheels, but are specially forged to fit the Singer's super-wide tyres. The exhaust is titanium and coated in ceramic.

The badges on the rear deck are made of 24-carat gold. Under the dash lurks all the tech a self-respecting modern nerd could need – nav, stereo, iPod connectivity – but neatly veiled behind period panels. Twenty-first century hardware hidden behind traditional charm: what more could you want?

Power? You can have just about as much as your wallet can handle. Hand over a vast enough cheque, and Singer will fit your 911 with a 3.9-litre flat-six of 1990s vintage, blueprinted and rebuilt using state-of-the-art components. Such an engine will make around 425bhp, seeing your old Neun-elfer to 62mph in a little under four seconds and on to a top speed over 175mph.

Driving a Singer quickly is a less puckering experience than that served up by traditional 911s, but an idiosyncratic one nonetheless. Despite the strengthening and modern components, you must never forget this is still a rear-wheel-drive with its engine in the very boot, one prone to bite your arm off if you push it too far. Handle with care: Singer can reinvent the past, but it can't reinvent physics.

SHELBY
MUSTANG
GT500

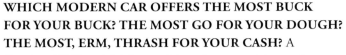

WHICH MODERN CAR OFFERS THE MOST BUCK FOR YOUR BUCK? THE MOST GO FOR YOUR DOUGH? THE MOST, ERM, THRASH FOR YOUR CASH? A Caterham R500 or Ariel Atom might stake strong claims to that crown, but if you're talking about brute horsepower for your dollar, it's tough to look much further than the Shelby Mustang GT500. For the equivalent of around £35,000, this bestriped brute serves up an absurd 662bhp from its 5.8-litre supercharged V8 – the most powerful road-going V8 in history, no less. So that's around 100bhp more than a Ferrari 458 Italia … for about a fifth of the price. This 'Stang might be the cheapest ticket into the 200mph club, too: after hitting 62mph in 3.7 seconds, the GT500 will top out, in a great flurry of hydrocarbons, at 202mph.

The GT500 is a fitting tribute to Carroll Shelby, the legendary Ford tuner and creator of some of the hottest Mustangs in history, not to mention the unforgettably terrifying AC Cobra. Shelby died in 2012 at the age of 89, but not before having a quick shot in the GT500. Apparently he rather liked it.

For some, the Mustang is – as Jeremy put it – a 'codpiece for the smaller gentleman', a brash lump of unsophisticated Americana. But to deride the 'Stang for wayward corners and its scratchy-plastic interior is to rather miss the point. The original pony car is, and always has been, about serving up a whole lotta power for not a whole lotta price.

'The power is always intoxicating,' grinned Clarkson when he blitzed the GT500 across France in a race against James and Richard on public transport. 'You never, ever get bored of that.'

But even 662 horses weren't enough to get JC to Milan ahead of the boys on the train: the first time in the history of *Top Gear*'s Big Races that public transport had beaten the car. Yeah, but can you do massive burnouts in a cross-continent locomotive?

FISKER

KARMA

IF YOU'RE (A) VERY RICH AND (B) ECO-MINDED, YOUR CHOICE OF THE AUTOMOTIVE PICK-AND-MIX IS CRUELLY LIMITED. Sure, you could slum it in a Prius, or opt for a mediumly frugal diesel Mercedes S-Class, but neither is likely to float your opulent, green boat. Which was where the Fisker Karma – the first car from the company of Henrik Fisker, the designer of the BMW Z8 and Aston Martin DB9 – came in.

Green? Unquestionably. The hybrid Karma – a car beloved of noted thespian and eco-campaigner Leonardo DiCaprio – boasted a solar panel on its roof, recycled glass paint and a tofu-worshipping range-extender powertrain. Though driven by electric motors, it had its own on-board power station: a GM-sourced 2.0-litre turbo petrol never feeding the wheels directly, only kicking in to generate extra current when the electric motors required it. Fully charged, it could manage around 50 miles before requiring a plug socket or calling on the petrol engine.

In all-electric stealth mode, the Karma was weirdly wonderful. Despite its enormo-dimensions – it shared a footprint with that Mercedes S-Class – the Fisker felt nimble and compact, its electric motor serving up its maximum 918lb·ft (no, seriously) of torque from a standstill. The Karma wasn't fun to drive in the traditional sense – no chance of lairy powerslides or precision apex-clipping here – but as a sensory experience it was addictive: simultaneously perfectly normal yet entirely strange, a big, leathery, luxury GT that could waft mile after mile of spooky, wafty silence.

Posh? Indeed. The Karma was as opulent as cars come, loaded to the brim with organic leather and gorgeous reclaimed wood. It cost a hefty £85,000.

Sadly, 'was' is the operative word here. Despite plans to sell 15,000 cars a year, Fisker folded in 2012. Back to the drawing board, billionaire greenies.

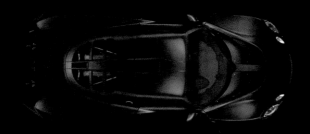

HENNESSEY

VENOM

JOHN HENNESSEY IS AN AMERICAN TUNER WHO LIKES MAKING CARS GO FAST. Traditionally the Texan has contented himself with upgrading Yank icons like the Viper and the Corvette, stuffing them with quadruple-figure power outputs and dragster-baiting quarter-mile times.

So when Hennessey turned his attentions to creating a 250mph-plus supercar, the result was never likely to be a half-baked effort. But maybe even Hennessey was surprised by the sheer lunacy of the Venom, an intoxicating combination of brute American muscle and the finesse of small-volume British sports-car manufacturing.

Here's how it happened. Starting with a Lotus Exige, Hennessy stretched the wheelbase by 60cm to make room for a twin-turbo 6.2-litre V8 making – wait for it – 1200bhp. So yes, that's Veyron SuperSport power in a car weighing half as much: 1270kg, to be precise. All going to the rear wheels. Which is an equation that balances itself with one very simple outcome: the most shocking, sustained acceleration of any road-going car in history.

To pin the throttle in the Venom is to be greeted with a savage headbutt by the horizon, a monstrous gush of boost shockingly savage in its delivery. Nought to 62mph takes somewhere around 2.5 seconds, with 200mph flashing barely 12 seconds later. The Veyron, by comparison, takes nearly nine seconds longer to reach the same speed. No road car in history has ever accelerated like this one. The Venom's top speed stands at a theoretical 275mph: Hennessey hasn't found a road long enough – and a pilot mad enough – to test whether this theory matches reality.

Scary? You'd better believe it. The Venom will spin its wheels at 200mph, and cheerily tear head from neck of any driver that doesn't afford it the reverence it demands. Which is an awful lot of reverence. Though its numbers may top the ubiquitous Bugatti, the Venom never set out to out-Veyron the Veyron. This is no accessible warp-speed car, a friendly way to spirit way past 200mph. The Venom is a raw, risk-laden racer: a grenade without the pin.

DODGE
VIPER

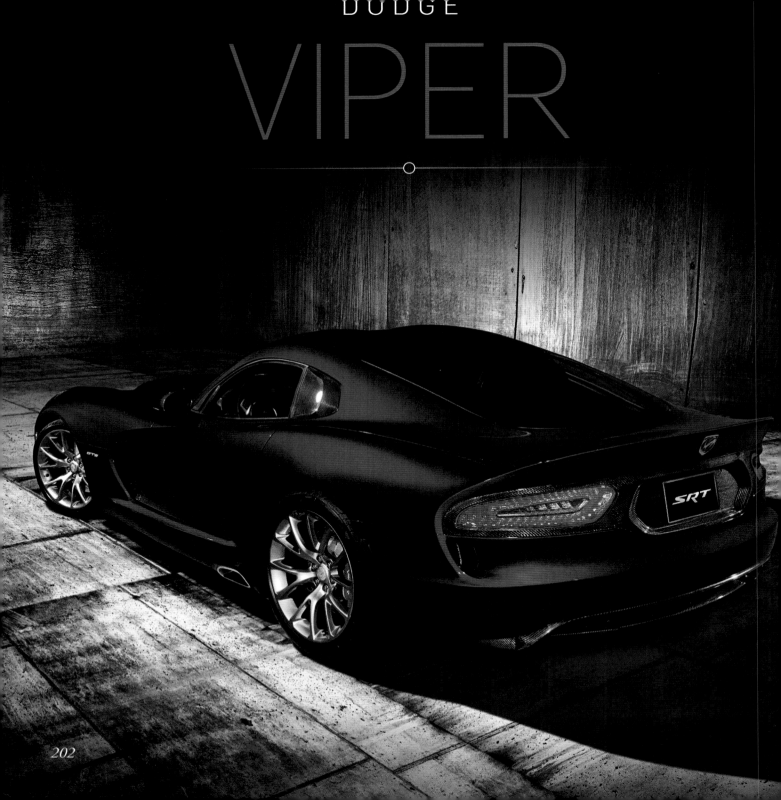

AIN'T NO REPLACEMENT FOR DISPLACEMENT.

So ran the philosophy of American muscle-car makers in the fifties and sixties, who jammed their simple wares with ever-larger V8s in a bid for road and track supremacy. Though the evolution of turbochargers, superchargers and even electric power has seen a move to downsizing in the twenty-first century, a few practitioners of the massive-engined, naturally aspirated formula remain.

And none more conspicuously than the Dodge Viper. Under that supertanker-length bonnet is stuffed an all-aluminium V10 engine, based on an ancient Lamborghini design and displacing no less than 8.4 litres. Or, to put it another way, more than five times the displacement of a 2014 Formula One engine. Sadly the Viper doesn't quite produce five times the power of an F1 car, but it's sufficiently potent nonetheless. The V10 churns out 640bhp, sufficient for a 0–62mph time of 3.7 seconds and a top speed of 208mph. That's faster than the Mercedes SLS with which the Viper shared its early development.

As befits its vast engine, the Viper has always cheerily represented the hammer-and-blowtorch end of the automotive engineering spectrum, but the latest iteration does feature at least a smattering of technology. There's adjustable stability control, two-mode suspension and even post-Iron-Age materials: the clamshell bonnet, roof and bootlid are all made of carbon fibre, lowering the Viper's mass. Oh, and launch control, because launch control makes all things better.

To drive? Well, how do you think a rear-drive sports car with an 8.4-litre engine is going to drive? The latest Viper isn't quite so paralysingly intimidating as its predecessors, but remains a visceral, uncensored experience, the sort of car you drive with furrowed brow, sweaty palms and at least two of the emergency services ready on speed dial. The McLaren P1, BMW i8 and others might have proved there is a replacement for displacement, but there's life in the old ways yet.

FORD

FIESTA ST

OFTEN THE SIMPLE THINGS IN LIFE ARE BEST.
Sure, a Michelin-starred main course of deconstructed guinea-fowl garnished with a pistachio foam and the atomized essence of Galapagos giant turtle may make the food critics swoon, but sometimes you just want … a decent bacon sandwich. Pig, bread and ketchup.

And that's what the Ford Fiesta ST is: a straightforward, no-frills, utterly satisfying bacon sandwich. The ingredients list is as yeoman as they come, a 1.6-litre turbocharged four-cylinder sending a far-from-stratospheric 180bhp to the front wheels though a six-speed manual gearbox, all wrapped up in a five-door, city-car shell.

Simple ingredients done right can result in subtle magic. Though this automotive pig roll is far from sizzlingly fast – nought to 62mph takes seven seconds, a figure within the grasp of even modest diesel saloons – it's bursting at the seams with vim and verve and vigour and many other happy words beginning with 'v'.

Every control tingles with energy, every journey becomes an event. The Ford Fiesta ST has, in the words of Mr James May, the fizz.

Lift off the accelerator in the middle of a corner, and the Fiesta will give an obliging twitch of its tail, just a hint that it'll behave with the vigorous, occasionally wayward vim of its 1980s hot-hatch predecessors rather than the predictable, somewhat stultifying manners of the modern crop. It's a happy throwback to the days when hot hatches were a little rough round the edges, wore their baseball caps backwards and slouchily smoked behind the bike sheds.

But for all its old-school charm, the Fiesta ST is very much of the zeitgeist. It'll officially manage nearly 50mpg and generate fewer emissions than a medium-sized cow. It won't anger militant greenists, nor – unless you drive it especially stupidly – your local traffic policeman. Throughout its life, its environmental footprint might well be smaller than that of a Toyota Prius. Old-school but entirely of the moment? Pass the ketchup …

THE REST OF THE WORLD

France. Japan. Sweden. Australia. All, according to the Top Gear Big Book Of History, former colonies of Britain, and all struggling to navigate their way through the modern world after being cut loose from Her Maj's mothership. But it turns out that, when they put their minds to it, these minor, backwater nations can build some surprisingly acceptable cars. France, after all, has cobbled together the Renaultsport Clio and Peugeot's Pikes Peak 208 in recent years. Japan has the awesome Lexus LFA and Nissan GT-R, while Sweden can boast Koenigsegg. Australia, as befits a nation that regards 'fire and outdoors' as a legitimate national cuisine, does a natty line in V8-stuffed pick-up trucks. Pray enjoy this poke around the wilder corners of the automotive globe.

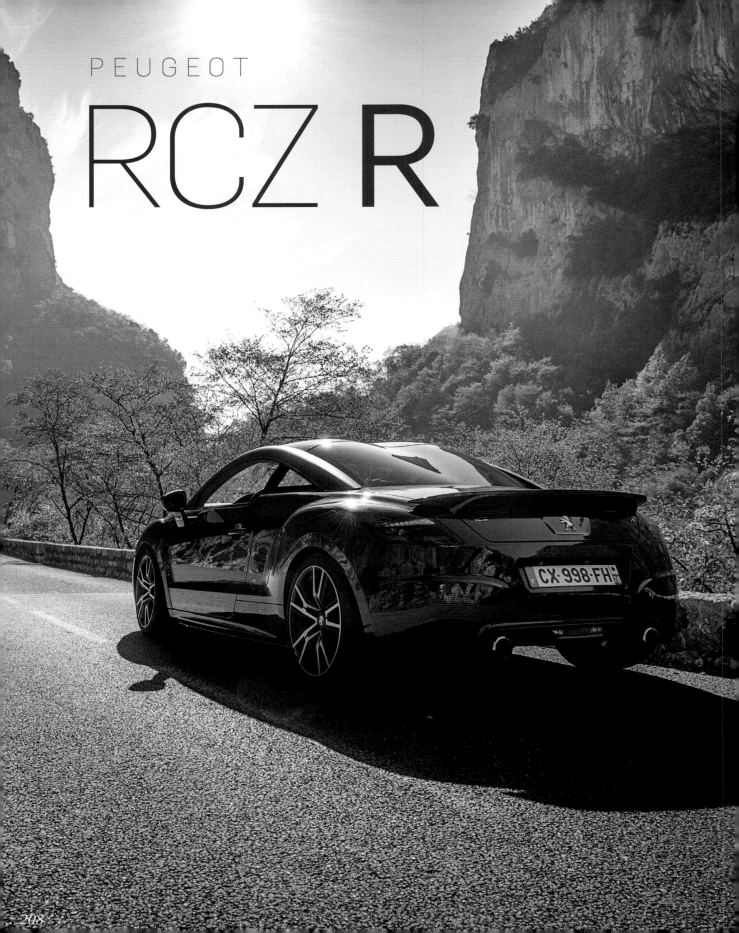

PEUGEOT
RCZ R

PROVIDED YOU DON'T CLASSIFY THE BUGATTI VEYRON AS FRENCH (which you shouldn't, because despite being built in Molsheim it's as German as leather trouserwear), the RCZ R is the most powerful French car of the twenty-first century. The hottest version of Peugeot's bubble-roofed coupé packs the most powerful 1.6-litre production engine in the world, a turbo four making 270bhp. That's a specific output of 168.75bhp per litre of displacement, more than even that pesky Veyron can muster.

It's also the first production model built by Peugeot Sport, Peugeot's Paris-based motorsport arm that was responsible for the 908 Le Mans racer and Seb Loeb's astonishing Pikes Peak 208. Squeezing 270bhp from a paltry 1598cc of displacement took plenty of Peugeot Sport's racing know-how. The 1.6-litre is treated to F1-spec aluminium pistons, a bespoke twin-scroll turbo, toughened conrods and low-friction bearings, which presumably means something to James May. Like the less potent RCZs, the R remains front-wheel drive, fed through a beefy six-speed manual gearbox. There's plenty of fast-car jewellery, too, from a fixed rear wing to bigger wheels and many shiny plaques and badges.

That combination of big turbo power and small coupé makes the RCZ R a damned effective point-and-squirt overtaker. The predictable slug of boost is backed by a surprising willingness to run to the redline, which means masses of power everywhere you want it, a muscular surge accompanied by a satisfying snort from the turbo. Through even the tightest corners, the RCZ R clings on hard, a differential between the front wheels stopping the nose from washing wide no matter how recklessly you pile into a hairpin.

OK, so the RCZ R's ride isn't exactly what you'd call forgiving, and more than 30 grand is a lot of money for what is, at heart, a small French coupé. But what price can you put on telling the next Veyron driver you meet that his or her engine is, pound for pound, a bit impotent?

GTBYCITROËN

IT IS NOT UNCOMMON FOR A CAR FROM THE REAL WORLD TO FIND ITS WAY INTO A VIDEO GAME.
But for a car to make the journey in the opposite direction is rather rarer. Yet that's exactly the story of the oddly named but undeniably spectacular GTByCitroën (yes, all one word). Designed by the French firm to star in *Grand Turismo 5* on the PlayStation, the GT's virtual unveiling led to such a clamorous reaction that Citroën decided to make its game-car real.

Which must have caused a few headaches, as the GTByCitroën was constructed around a hypothetical hydrogen powertrain, employing techniques and materials from the land of science fiction, not production reality.

So how was it possible to make it real? Well, extravagant as its visuals and materials may have been, the console-based GT was at least grounded in the reality of physics. The swooping bodywork is built with aerodynamic efficiency in mind: those gaping front air intakes and

gigantic carbon diffuser acting to minimize lift and drag.

The GT's interior – accessed through Mercedes SLS-style gullwing doors – is a strange mix of race, retro and ridiculous. Bucket seats and a head-up display offer a concession to modernity, but around those are wrapped great swathes of copper, both polished and rough. It shouldn't work, especially not in a supercar apparently hailing from several centuries into the future, but somehow it does.

And what about that hydrogen powertrain? Perhaps sensibly, for real-world service Citroën switched the GT's hypothetical fuel cell for a far more conventional engine: a dirty great V8. Did it work? You bet it did: noisier than the Apocalypse, fast enough to cause lasting damage to your face, and perhaps the only machine on the planet that can make Pagani Huayras and Lamborghini Aventadors look sensible and understated, the GTByCitroën brought London to a standstill in the hands of *Top Gear*. What a pity Citroën only built one …

CLIO 200

THE CLIO 22 REPRESENTS THE END OF AN ERA. It is one of the very last of the naturally aspirated hot hatches, a bundle of fizz and energy that does without turbocharging or, heaven forbid, electric power in favour of a good, old-fashioned, high-revving engine. It's also perhaps the greatest hot hatch of the twenty-first century, and one of the very best of all time.

In this case, that good, old-fashioned, high-revving engine is a 2.0-litre four-cylinder making 197bhp. That's not a vast amount of power in a world of 276bhp Peugeot RCZs and 354bhp Mercedes A45 AMGs, but the Clio 200 is about much more than raw stats (though, for the record, these stand at 6.9 seconds for the 0–62mph run, and a top speed of 141mph). It's about a car that feels virtually wired into your nervous system, one that responds to every input with such immediacy and precision it's as if the car is an extension of your own body.

Eschewing turbocharging means the response of the Clio's engine is perfectly linear: there's no waiting for turbines to spool up, or trying to keep the motor in its 'sweet spot'. That said, if you're used to driving a turbo petrol or diesel, at first the Clio 200 can feel rather anaemic, lacking in power. The trick is to slot it a gear or two below the one you think you should be in: this engine does its best work north of 5000rpm, climbing to a raucous scream as you pile towards its 7250rpm redline. The steering is pin-sharp, the Clio changing direction with the twitching immediacy of a rat terrier. It's not relaxing to drive, but it's mighty exhilarating.

Hustling this simple, effervescent little Clio along a winding country lane remains perhaps the defining hot-hatch experience of the twenty-first century. Other hot hatches may be quicker, or more technologically advanced, but none has ever been quite so fizzy.

PEUGEOT
ONYX

THE PEUGEOT ONYX CONCEPT IS MADE OF PAPER. AND FELT. And also copper. No, this isn't the most ambitious *Blue Peter* project in history, but rather Peugeot's effort to show that there's a world of automotive materials beyond steel, aluminium, plastic and leather.

So those coppery-looking body panels are *real* copper – untreated, raw, almost a millimetre thick and handbeaten into shape by a craftsman. Peugeot says the colour of the copper changes over time as it oxidizes with the air. So chunks of your Onyx might even end up green. The fuel tank is made of blown crystal, while the interior is trimmed in felt – or boiled wool, to use its more prosaic name.

The paper? That's the stuff forming the Onyx's dash and door top, the stuff that looks like wood, right down to the grain and texture. In fact it's recycled newspaper, pressed together with enough force to turn it back into

wood – of sorts – that can be cut, milled and carved, just like real timber. Look very closely, though, and you can see the remnants of printed words and letters.

All of which might make the Onyx sound like a pie-in-the-sky concept, dreamed up by designers never to see light outside of a motorshow stand. However, this bizarre Peugeot is not only real, but drives too. And it drives fast, using the V8 and gearbox from Peugeot's 908 Le Mans project – a 3.7-litre diesel producing an eye-watering 600bhp – supplemented with a hybrid module because, y'know, a Le Mans engine just isn't fast enough, is it? In a car weighing just 1100kg thanks to a carbon fibre chassis, that's a recipe for some acceleration explosive enough to … well, to boil wool and turn newspaper into wood.

Sadly Peugeot says it won't put the Onyx into production, but will use it to inform its future road cars. A 600bhp diesel 208 hot hatch made of copper and back copies of the *Daily Star*? Why not?

PEUGEOT
208 T16

**EVERY MOTORSPORT SERIES IN THE WORLD –
F1, WRC, NASCAR, YOU NAME IT** – is bound by an
encyclopaedia-thick book of regulations and laws determining the
size, shape, weight, power and almost every other aspect of the
cars permitted to race.

But what if you could build a race car that had to adhere to
not one single regulation? A car with just one goal: to tackle a
mountain road faster than anything in history. That was the aim
of Peugeot's 208 T16, a bespoke racer built to compete in the
legendary Pikes Peak hillclimb in 2013.

The Pikes mountain is legendary and lethal, a 12.4-mile Colorado
tarmac track winding from 1440 metres to over 4300 at the summit,
a course of no less than 156 corners and fearsome, 1000-foot drops.
And for one weekend each summer, it's turned into the world's
wildest race-track as hundreds of fearless/stupid drivers try to get
their no-limits racers to the top as fast as possible. Peugeot's not-
so-secret weapon? An insanely, short, wide, powerful … thing. The

Pikes Peak car was a 208 in name and silhouette only: beneath its
carbon fibre bodywork sits a spaceframe chassis wrapped around a
3.2-litre V6, boosted to a sofa-chewing 875bhp with the addition
of the turbocharger from Peugeot's Le Mans racer. The T16 weighs
just 875kg, which, as the maths-inclined may notice, gives it a very
neat power-to-weight ratio of exactly one horsepower per kilogram.
Nuclear warheads have packed less potency.

And then all Peugeot needed was a man capable of driving the
thing. So they called up a bloke called Seb Loeb, a fairly handy
driver with just the nine World Rally Championship titles under
his belt, who said, 'Yeah, I'm free that weekend, why not?'

So how did it do? Not too shabbily. Peugeot's aim was to break
the Pikes course record, which stood at 9 minutes, 46.1 seconds.
Their time? 8 minutes, 13.9 seconds. Loeb didn't just beat the
record, he obliterated it. Smashed it into a million little pieces,
carved more than 90 seconds from it. Amazing what you can do
when you don't have to play by the rules.

C8 LAVIOLETTE

HOLLAND LEADS THE WORLD IN MANY FIELDS. Clogs. Tulips. Mind-altering coffee shops. But not, traditionally, supercars. Or any cars at all, in fact.

So if you're going to announce your nation's presence on the supercar stage, how better to do it than with a bright orange, V8-powered slice of utter insanity, a car with the strangest, most glorious cabin this side of a Pagani Huayra, a car surely cooked up after a long afternoon in one of those aforementioned coffee shops?

Certainly you couldn't imagine the Spyker C8 Laviolette emerging from, say, Germany or Japan. Just look at that cockpit: banks and banks of stainless toggles, a great horizontal bar of exposed gearchange, even a red 'safety cover' you must flip up before firing the engine start button. Over the top? Unquestionably. Rather wonderful? That too.

Under the chrome and orange, the Spyker is a reasonably straightforward supercar. Behind the driver sits a 4.2-litre V8 borrowed from Audi, driving the rear wheels though an automatic gearbox. It's built about an all-aluminium spaceframe – manufactured in Coventry, of all places – and the suspension is designed and supplied by Lotus.

All promising stuff, but between a lazy gearbox and less-than-lissom kerbweight, the C8 feels brisk rather than outright quick: 0–62mph takes 4.5 seconds, with a top speed of 186mph. And it costs nearly £200,000. Yes, it drives neatly, but for half that money you could have a serious sports car – a Porsche 911 or Audi R8, to name but two – that would leave it for dust down any road or track.

But you don't buy a C8 Laviolette to teach Porsche and Audi drivers a lesson round a circuit. You buy it for its celebration of sheer decadence. This is a cartoonish chunk of life-affirming insanity that proves the world of supercars isn't all about numbers and acceleration. It's very expensive, very silly and very, very orange. A genuine slice of Dutch courage.

VOLVO

C30 POLESTAR

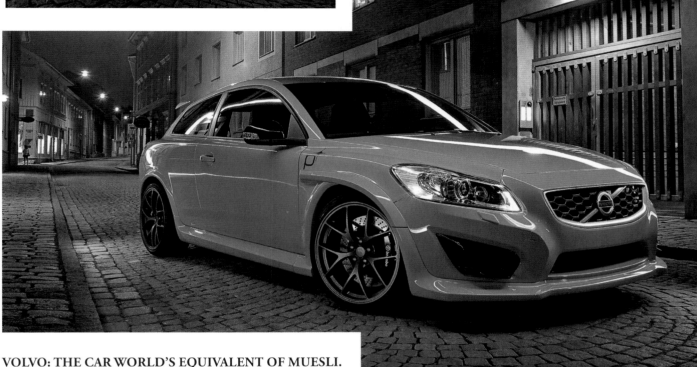

VOLVO: THE CAR WORLD'S EQUIVALENT OF MUESLI.

Or contents insurance. Grown-up, probably a good idea, but fundamentally a bit dull.

Unless, that is, you're talking about the C30 Polestar, a car Jeremy called 'a deafening, electric-blue streak from the frozen north'. This is a 400bhp, 4WD maniac of a hot hatch – proof that Volvo, when it takes a break from all the safety tech and capacious estates, can do silly as well as sensible.

Engineered with the assistance of the race team that runs Volvo's Swedish touring car effort, the C30 Polestar uses the 2.5-litre five-cylinder turbo from the last Ford Focus RS, but with tougher pistons and conrods and a new turbo to achieve that BMW-rivalling power output. It sits lower to the road than the stock C30, with race-grade springs and dampers and a very functional bodykit.

The Polestar needs every one of its chassis and aero upgrades, for this is a supercar-bothering hot hatch. Nought to 62mph

takes somewhere around four seconds, and that four-wheel-drive system offers up phenomenal traction in any conditions. There's barely any turbo lag, that five-pot emitting a screaming, half-an-F1-car soundtrack, a splitting metallic wail that permeates the cabin and buzzes your brain into a happy soup of adrenal goo.

But here's the best bit about the Polestar. Yes, it's mad-quick, and yes, it'll turn your ears to pulp, but it still feels thoroughly Volvo-ish and unbreakable: a Scandi-grade, road-ready hot hatch rather than the concept it is. Because that's the only real downside to this hottest of hot hatches. It existed as a one-off, a car to demonstrate that Volvo still has a silly side. Sadly it never reached production. Which, all things considered, is rather a shame. Clarkson agreed. 'It is genuinely remarkable,' he said when he tested it round a sodden *Top Gear* track. 'Really fast, really hard, really raw. And it goes like the clappers …'

KOENIGSEGG

AGERA

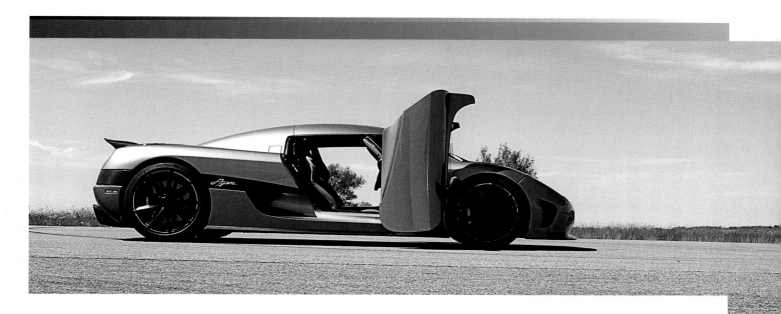

EVEN THE STIG HIMSELF WOULDN'T DESCRIBE THE AGERA'S PREDECESSOR – the 805bhp Koenigsegg CCX – as a car that needed any more power. After all, that was the car that nearly assassinated the white-suited one, punting him into a tyre wall as he gunned for a Power Lap record back in 2006, an incident that led to the CCX gaining its patented '*Top Gear* wing'.

But, clearly deciding the CCX wasn't anything like intimidating enough, Swedish firm Koenigsegg gave its successor even sharper teeth. The new-from-the-ground-up Agera ditched the CCX's supercharged V8 in favour of a new twin-turbo eight-cylinder monster, an engine making a massive 905bhp.

The Agera got more visual bite, too. Its front end is wider, the ram air inlets beneath the lights are redesigned, its sills wider. Its rear, too, shares little with the CCX, boasting new LED lights and the mother of all rear diffusers. Yes, it carries the DNA of its predecessor, but the Agera is more modern, more aggressive. More scary. It's also a more efficient

shape, creating about 30 per cent more downforce front and rear, which equates to some 300kg at 150mph.

There's a gorgeous centre console, with elegant backlit switches beneath a hi-res touchscreen. Here you can adjust functions such as nav and audio, as well as settings like gearshift and traction control. Very high-tech, very cool.

As are the doors. To get into the Agera, you first touch a small rubber button below the door sill, which sees the window scroll down an inch, and the door pop open with a gentle crack. Lift gently and it swings up and forward effortlessly in a clean, smooth arc. Lower yourself over the wide sill and deep into the racing bucket seat, and you'll find yourself in the perfect driving position, with a view through the narrow windscreen like that of a Le Mans prototype.

Hit the starter button and the Agera fires with a wail, waves of sonic V8 shrapnel reverberating off the scenery. It's the sound of a race car, all mechanical chatter and clatter, a coarse

contrast to the plush, futuristic surroundings of the cabin. Clunk the left-hand paddle to shift the sequential box into first gear, squeeze the throttle, and the Agera pulls away with the civility of a hot hatch. But boot the accelerator, and the Agera's pair of turbos take just long enough to spool up to allow you to register the thought: '910bhp? Well, this doesn't seem that fa—' before the V8 grabs 3000rpm and the Agera takes off like a fighter jet on full afterburner. It is savage, physically shocking acceleration that leaves you mute, gurning as the numbers on the digital display spool up with impossible speed.

When the Agera arrived, its closest rival was probably the Pagani Zonda: a similarly low-volume, hugely expensive creation from a similarly youthful newcomer to the hypercar world. But the Zonda and Agera are as different as chalk and, say, Mickey Rourke with toothache and a severe hangover. Where the Zonda – or even, say, Lamborghini's Aventador – releases its power in a smooth, even flow, the Agera detonates like a 3000lb bomb.

But as you acclimatize to the magnitude of the experience, the Agera reveals itself to be more than a simple warhead. The steering, so light at low speeds, is quick and intuitive at pace, imbuing the Agera with surprising nimbleness for a two-metre-wide hypercar. The near-race-spec suspension soaks up bumps with astonishing ease. No, the Agera doesn't match that Zonda – or, indeed, the Bugatti Veyron – for sheer ease and usability. It doesn't try to: the Koenigsegg experience is far more visceral than that. But it is also much more sophisticated than its fission-spec powertrain suggests.

And faster than almost anything else on the planet. In fact, the Agera might just be the fastest road car ever created. 62mph comes up in 3.1 seconds, and 124mph in 8.9 seconds. Top speed? Somewhere north of 250mph, and perhaps even further north than the Bugatti SuperSport's 268mph. At least, that's what Koenigsegg's modelling says: the Swedes haven't built a runway long enough to discover the Agera's true v-max yet …

HSV
MALOO

WE'VE ALL BEEN THERE. You've a dozen piglets to transport to a fair in the next county, and not enough time in which to get there. Normally, of course, you'd take your Audi RS6 Avant, but you don't want to get pig-mess all over that nice leather upholstery. What to do?

Easy. Crank the HSV Maloo out of the garage. This farmers' favourite is a 425bhp, V8-powered pick-up truck, a ute that could hail from only one country: Down Under.

Specifically from Holden Special Vehicles, the performance wing of General Motors' Australian operation. Which means the Maloo uses the same GM-sourced V8 found in the Vauxhall VXR8 (in fact, save for the flatbed in place of the rear seats and boot, the Maloo is an identical twin of Vauxhall's smoky saloon). It's an engine potent enough to turn your crate of piglets in the boot straight to thin-sliced bacon: the Maloo will do 0–62mph in 4.9 seconds, and squeal onwards to a limited 155mph.

And, should you decide you want a smoky hint to that bacon, the Maloo will happily turn its rear tyres into acrid rubber-clouds. With several furlongs between front and rear axle, the Maloo slides – in a capable pair of hands at least – with elegant predictability, requiring marginally less bravery than stubby supercars. And when you've finished sliding round the track, you can plug a USB stick into a port in the glovebox to extract a full record of your misdemeanours, including G-force oversteer angles. These numbers will be quite large and potentially incriminating.

And here's a *Top Gear* top tip for you: if you *do* use the Maloo for transporting piglets – or, indeed, any other commercial livestock of your choosing – the taxman will classify it as a commercial vehicle, allowing you to claim the tax back. Which means you can have this 425bhp truck for £40,000, which is a whole lot of power and load-lugging ability for the cash. Strewth.

HONDA CIVIC
TYPE R

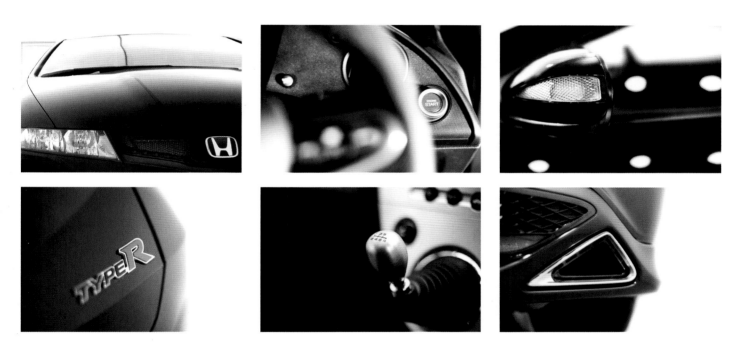

THE CIVIC TYPE R WAS NEVER THE MOST GROWN-UP OR UNDERSTATED OF HOT HATCHES. Even the standard Civic upon which it was based – with its dashboard from the Romulans and door handles from a post-war fridge – looked like a 1950s vision of the distant future. The Type R added a massive bodykit, big wheels, a fat rear wing, deep-dish steering wheel and wingback bucket seats. Subtle? Not at all. Childishly brilliant? Definitely.

But far more important than its childishly brilliant appearance was what lurked under the Type R's pointy bonnet. Roundly ignoring the hot-hatch world's shift towards turbocharged engines, Honda stuck with what it did best: a 2.0-litre atmospheric four-cylinder with its famed 'VTEC' variable valve timing, a 197bhp engine capable of spinning right the way to 8000rpm.

As is the proper hot-hatch way, the Type R pushed that power to the front wheels through a pleasingly snappy six-speed manual gearbox. By modern fast-hatch standards, it wasn't absurdly quick – nought to 62mph took 6.5 seconds, with a 146mph top speed. But when that engine climbed up past 5000rpm and clicked into its screaming VTEC phase, the Type R entered a higher plane of hot-hatch happiness, churning its way to the lofty redline in a ball of naturally aspirated noise and pleasingly precise handling.

'Its engine spins so fast, it generates its own little gravity field!' exclaimed Clarkson when he tested the Type R. No-one does engines like Honda, and this is one of its best. Truth be told, Jeremy wasn't quite so enamoured by the fizzy little Civic as the rest of us, declaring its suspension less sophisticated than that of its Type R predecessor. Then again, he's not *always* right, the big man. With even Honda later conceding that its hot hatches had to go turbo, this Civic Type R was the last of a very, very fine breed.

TOYOTA

HILUX

'WHAT DO YOU HAVE TO DO TO KILL ONE?' ASKED CLARKSON IN EXASPERATION. We've crashed them into trees, drowned them in seawater, dropped caravans on them, hit them with wrecking balls, set them on fire and even exploded entire blocks of flats around them, but still the Hiluxes survive. When humanity is destroyed in a nuclear apocalypse, and the surface of earth reduced to dust, this no-frills pick-up will still be trundling happily around. This is the cockroach of the car world, a ute that cannot be destroyed by fire, water or large quantities of gravity.

Which makes the Hilux not only the ideal specimen for performing cruel and unusual car experiments upon, but also the weapon of choice for farmers, adventurers and small-scale armies around the world. From the Amazonian basin to the heights of the Himalayas, wherever on earth you find humans, you'll likely find a battered Hilux not far behind. For a pick-up that can

survive Clarkson, safe to say a bit of swamp, glacier or assault by enemy fire is all in a day's work.

As is bumbling to the North Pole. It was, of course, a Hilux that Jeremy and James relied upon to carry them to the top of the world quicker than Hammond and his pack of dogs. OK, so the Toyota got a few modifications for Arctic duty – most notably a vast set of snow-tyres and James's bumper-based 'toilet solution' – but the Polar Hilux conquered the toughest terrain on earth without a cough or stumble.

Throw in its sterling work as Clarkson's amphibious 'Toybota', and ferrying Captain Slow to the very edge of Iceland's most active volcano, and the Hilux can justifiably claim to be the most important car in the history of *Top Gear*. Certainly it's the toughest to kill.

MAZDA

FURAI

236

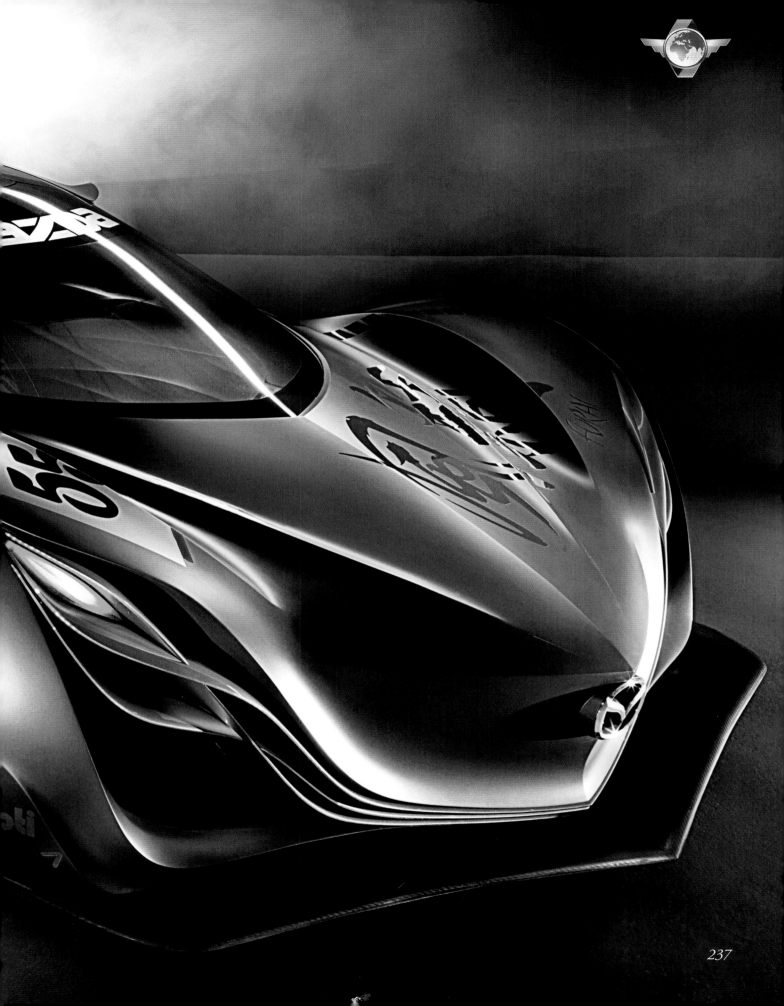

CONCEPT CARS ARE NOT USUALLY MADE TO BE DRIVEN.

Concept cars are created as design exercises for motor shows, showpieces to demonstrate a marque's future styling direction. Concept cars sit on plinths under glittering lights, spinning helplessly like rotisserie chickens. They usually weigh many dozens of tonnes, because they're built on daft chassis that don't have to steer or even roll, and sometimes even made of clay. More often than not, concept cars don't have an engine.

But not the Mazda Furai. Cooked up to showcase Mazda's Nagare design language, this is no trailer queen, but a bloody serious race car. Under that extraordinary skin lurks a 460bhp rotary-engined Le Mans prototype, running on E100 ethanol. It wears the number '55' in honour of Mazda's winner of the 1991 24 Hours of Le Mans, the legendary 787B.

The racing reference is more than mere lip service. The Furai's body is sculpted with Computational Fluid Dynamics (CFD), the technique favoured by money-no-object F1 teams. Which means it's not only stunning but aerodynamically efficient: every wing, fin and vent is there for function, not fancy. Look at those fantastic sweeping lines running up and around the headlights, at the alloy blade mirrors on top of the door, the sculpting of the body. 'It's really important that we create some cars that end up on an eight-year-old kid's bedroom wall,' Furai designer Laurens van den Acker told *Top Gear* at the car's unveiling. 'People don't dream enough any more.'

The Furai's cockpit is just as redolent of Le Mans fantasy. There are no instruments on the dash: all the information you need is provided by the LCD screen on the steering wheel, which also has change-up lights stretched across the top of its rim, and gearshift paddles mounted on either side, which click with microscopic, military-grade precision.

But the magnificent bodywork isn't the most incredible thing about the Furai. That honour is reserved for the noise from that rotary engine: a buzzing, high-pitching stabbing staccato, a mixture of killer bee and buzzsaw that climbs to a demented cackle as the Furai accelerates. Which, with just 675kg – only a few kilos more than an F1 car – to be shoved by that 460bhp of race-bred power, it does mighty quickly indeed.

Pin the throttle and the Furai's revs build with astonishing pace, those little steering-wheel lights blinking quicker than you could possibly imagine. Near the 8800rpm limiter, click the right paddle to move up through the six-speed sequential box, and the next gear is engaged in a microsecond with a forceful thump. With no let-up in acceleration through second, third or even fourth gear, your helmet – because you can't drive the Furai without one – is pinned back into the headrest. Nought to 60mph takes less than three seconds, while top speed stands at 180mph. Through the bends, the Furai will pull three lateral Gs, all those wings and diffusers offering huge downforce to help the Mazda tackle corners like a genuine race car. Which, of course, it is. Stopping is just as physical, the track-spec brakes thumping you forwards in your belts as the Furai drags itself back from triple-figure speeds to a standstill as quickly as it got there. The Furai is not just the best-driving concept car in history, but one of the best-driving cars, full-stop.

Or, rather, we should say '*was* not just the best-driving concept car', because the Furai, sadly, is no more. Just one car was ever built, a car heartbreakingly destroyed by fire during a *Top Gear* photoshoot (it wasn't our fault, honest – the man from Mazda was driving), a lick of flame from the exhaust catching and chargrilling the bodywork before the fire crews could arrive. It was an ignominious end to the Furai story, but if any concept car deserves to rise from the ashes, it is this one.

NISSAN

GT-R

HAS ANY CAR IN HISTORY EVER OFFERED MORE BANG FOR YOUR BUCK THAN THE 'R34' NISSAN GT-R? As Jeremy proved, the car the Japanese call 'Godzilla' is faster than a bullet train, fast enough to cause permanent damage to human necks. The GT-R will get round the Nurburgring quicker than a Porsche 911 Turbo, and go down a greasy back-road more rapidly than almost anything else on earth. And all this from a car that costs little more than a heavily optioned Audi A6.

GT-Rs of the past were hopped-up versions of Nissan's sensible Skyline, the Japanese equivalent of, say, a BMW M3. But the GT-R is a custom-built supercar. Up front stands a 3.8-litre twin-turbo V8 pumping around 600bhp though a very clever dual-clutch gearbox and even cleverer four-wheel-drive system. Chuck in launch control and a mind-boggling electronic brain that can adjust the shock absorbers and differentials every hundredth of a second to keep the GT-R in optimal attack mode, and you're looking at a formula for serious brain-melting pace.

'The acceleration is just blistering!' yelled Clarkson when he tested the GT-R around Japan's Suzuka circuit. 'It's just savage!'

The GT-R will rocket from nought to 62mph in around three seconds, and keep running to nearly 200mph: proper hypercar statistics. But even more astonishing than its straight-line performance is what it can do through the bends. 'This was built to mash your mind in the corners,' explained Clarkson shortly before the GT-R, well, mashed his mind in the corners. In fact, the GT-R generates such vicious G-force in the bends that each wheel has a special 'knurling' on the rim to stop the tyres from ripping off. 'I wish my collar had a knurled rim,' groaned JC as the Nissan inflicted yet more pain on him. 'It would stop my head from coming off.'

The GT-R isn't beautiful, at least not in the conventional sense. In fact, it looks like a discordant mess, but every crease and every angle is there to channel air to that huge rear spoiler. Some have argued that, with all its electronic assistance, the GT-R offers nothing more than a digital, video-game experience, but Clarkson begs to differ. 'It feels mechanical,' says the big man. 'It feels analogue. It feels fan-bleeding-tastic!'

HONDA
FCX CLARITY

JAMES MAY, A MAN NOT GIVEN TO IDLE OVERSTATEMENT, CALLED IT THE MOST IMPORTANT CAR SINCE THE CAR WAS INVENTED, DECLARING THE FCX CLARITY NOTHING LESS THAN THE FUTURE OF MOTORING.

Which is a bold claim for something that looks, well, like a car. The FCX doesn't drive itself. It doesn't levitate. It does 0–60mph in a very conventional nine seconds, and has an equally conventional top speed around 100mph.

So far, so very normal. So what's so different about the FCX? Well, it's an electric car, but not like any electric car that has gone before. The FCX's front wheels are driven by an electric motor, but – unlike in, say, the Nissan Leaf – this doesn't draw its power from a stack of boot-floor batteries. This car has its own, on-board, electricity generation station: a station that takes the form of a hydrogen fuel cell.

As in your Ford Focus, at the back of the FCX sits a fuel tank. But instead of filling it with petrol or diesel, you pump the Honda with compressed, liquid hydrogen. This is combined with oxygen in the fuel cell, which, in a complicated and boring way, produces electricity. That electricity is then used to drive the motor, which turns the front wheels. Very simple, but, at the same time, very clever. While battery-powered electric cars struggle to do more than 100 miles – and often far less – on a charge, and then require several hours to replenish their batteries, the FCX will go 270 miles on a tank and, if you can find a hydrogen filling station nearby, can be fully refuelled in just a few minutes. And, unlike petrol, hydrogen will never run out: it's the most abundant element in the universe. All that's required now is for the hydrogen infrastructure to catch up with technology. Which is taking, ahem, a little longer than expected. The future of motoring? We're still waiting to find out …

LEXUS

LFA

LEXUS IS THE LIBRARIAN OF THE CAR WORLD. This is not *necessarily* an insult, because bookish, beige Lexus does many things well. Lentilmatic hybrid engines, for one. Consistent panel gaps. And dullness. Lexus does dullness very well.

Which is why, when Toyota's posh division announced it was making a supercar, there was more than a little scepticism expressed. Especially when it became clear just what a nutjob of a supercar the LFA would be.

The carbon fibre LFA is a million miles removed from its sensible-shoed Lexus brethren. It is a slavering loon, a sharp-toothed, bona fide supercar. And it is very definitely not a hybrid: in fact, the LFA is powered by a 4.8-litre, 552bhp V10 engine that's as light as a V6 and revs so fast that Lexus had to fit a virtual rev counter. A conventional analogue needle couldn't keep pace with the speed at which the V10 gains and loses revs.

There's more geektastic detail, too. The flappy paddle to the right of the wheel, the one that sends you up through the six-paddle-speed gearbox, has a slightly lighter action than the left-hand paddle to change down, just so you know you're heading in the right direction. The mirrors are specially shaped to funnel air into the vents above the rear wheels. And the gap above the badge at the front edge of the bonnet is not a sign of shoddy build quality – this is *Lexus*, after all – but a specially designed air intake.

The result of all the power and cleverness is a supercar-worthy set of stats: 0–62mph in 3.7 seconds and a top speed north of 202mph. But does it *feel* like a supercar? In a word … yes.

'That's explosive!' grinned Hammond as he thrashed the LFA round the TG test track, pursued by a laser-firing spaceship (no, we're not sure either). 'It's … immediate!'

The rear-drive LFA boasts true supercar handling, too. Get it wrong and it takes absolutely no prisoners. But get it right and you'll be laughing. At least, you will if you're not the one who had to actually buy the thing: the LFA wears the decidedly un-Lexus price tag of £340,000 …

MITSUBISHI

EVO X

FROM THE VERY TURN OF THE MILLENNIUM, THE MITSUBISHI EVO HAS BEEN LOCKED IN UNENDING COMBAT with Subaru's Impreza WRX STI for four-wheel-drive, rally-saloon supremacy. Generations have come and gone, with Mitsubishi claiming victory one year only for Subaru to return with a yet-faster, yet-grippier Impreza. And then the Evo would go faster still, and … well, you get the picture. Of all the Evo–Impreza knockout blows delivered, perhaps the most thumping was struck by the Evo X when Jeremy tested it against 2008's Impreza WRX STi . The result wasn't so much a thorough beating as a ritual humiliation for the Scooby, a result perhaps unsurprising when you realize exactly how much tech the monster Mitsu was packing.

The Evo X boasted not only a turbocharged 2.0-litre engine churning out 276bhp, but the most baffling array of four-wheel-drive acronyms to keep it stuck to the road: Super All Wheel Control (S-AWC), Active Centre Differential (ACD), Active Yaw Control (AYC) and Active Stability Control (ASC). To understand how all these work would require a postgraduate doctorate in astrophysics – hell, even Jeremy had to resort to the handbook – but what it means in practical terms is this: a car with obscene pace and traction on any surface, at any speed. If you're very brave or very stupid, the Evo can be coaxed into the most mammoth four-wheel drifts, but most of the time it prefers to cling on like a needy barnacle. It does exactly what you want it to do, even if you have no real idea how it's doing it.

It's an utterly functional-looking thing, with ducts to feed in cooling air, and intakes behind the front wheel arches to allow hot air to escape from the engine bay. There's even a 'twist' in the rear spoiler to assist airflow and maximize downforce. The interior, on the other hand, keeps things brutally simple: wheel, pedals, a few dials and that's your lot. But who needs keyless entry or traffic-sensing sat navs when you've got a rally-bred super-saloon capable of giving a Ferrari a bloody nose?

'I thought it would be impossible to make a four-door saloon more exciting than the Evo IX,' cooed Clarkson. 'But with the X, they have.'

And, after JC's test, the Evo X got even quicker: in final 'FQ400' guise, it made very nearly 400bhp. It's never been officially confirmed what the 'FQ' stands for, but it's generally acknowledged the second word is 'quick' and the first is an, um, Anglo-Saxon adjective …

IMPREZA
CS400
COSWORTH

AFTER ITS 'STANDARD' IMPREZA STI TOOK A
THOROUGH BEATING AT THE HANDS OF THE
MITSUBISHI EVO X AND MR CLARKSON, Subaru decided
drastic action must be taken to restore respectability to its rally
icon. So it handed over the STI to the tuning boffins at Cosworth:
boffins better known for their sterling work with hot Fords.

Proving they're equally at home with Japanese horsepower,
Cosworth stripped the 2.5-litre flat-four engine back to
its undies, changing the turbo, rods and pistons, and
strengthening everything that could possibly be strengthened.
The result? A 33 per cent jump in power to a nice round
400bhp, reaching all four wheels through Subaru's clever
centre differential. Good thing, with all that extra power,
that Cosworth also upgraded the gearbox, and fitted the
STI with huge racing brakes and beefier springs.

Cosworth's fettling created a four-wheel-drive hot hatch with
performance to rival a Gallardo: 0–62mph took 3.5 seconds,
with top speed limited to 155mph. The way the Cossie delivered
its power was far from subtle, all those horses arriving in a single
huge hit after a long pause for turbo lag, but was undeniably
addictive. And once that engine spooled up, the CS400 was
pretty much untouchable on road or track, with huge grip no
matter what the road threw at it, delicious steering feel and a
glorious thrum from that four-cylinder engine as its needle honed
in on the limiter. Set the differential to 'silly bugger' mode and
it would even exit a corner with a neat wag from its tail. All the
ability of a rally car, with a reasonable measure of sophistication.

The perfect real-world supercar, then? Not quite. Trouble
was, the Impreza CS400 cost a puckering £50,000 (and
Subaru admitted – with a limited run of just 75 cars – even
that pricey ticket didn't cover the engineering costs). That's
a lot of cash for an ugly Japanese hatchback with a hole
in its nose. But as an all-guns-blazing sally in the Subaru–
Mitsubishi war, the Cosworth did its job. One-all, Mitsu …

HONDA
MEAN
MOWER

THE RELENTLESS MARCH OF TECHNOLOGY HAS HELPED SPEED UP MANY ASPECTS OF EVERYDAY LIFE IN THE TWENTY-FIRST CENTURY, from paying for your groceries to transferring the contents of your bank account to a recently deposed Nigerian prince. Apart from one: cutting your lawn. Though mankind can send a vehicle to Mars, we hadn't figured out a way to make trimming the grass a less plodding, adrenaline-sapping affair.

Until, that is, Honda teamed up with touring car outfit Team Dynamics to build Stig a 130mph ride-on mower. Does our tame racing driver have a garden? Is he aware of the concept of grass? We have no idea.

Anyhow. At the strimmer's heart was a 109bhp engine from a Honda VTR FireStorm, and if that doesn't sound like a whole lot of power, consider the Mean Mower weighs just 140kg. Even with a driver on board, you're looking at a garden tool with a power-to-weight ratio of well over 500bhp per tonne. Which is more than a Caterham R500. The Lord's outfield wouldn't know what hit it.

Because, though built around a race-style spaceframe chassis and capable of slicing from nought to 60mph in around four seconds, this is still a bona fide grass-slayer. The Mean Mower packs two 4000rpm electric motors armed with metal brake cables to flay the green stuff into submission.

But on the track rather than the Lord's outfield, the Mean Mower is, as you might guess, something of a grass-scented handful to drive. This is a terrifying, twitchy little thing to push hard, launching forward with not a hint of slack and a ridiculous din from the side-mounted exhaust, an evil combination of nuclear explosion and machine gun accompanied by a barrage of blue flame. Alan Titchmarsh, we fear, would not approve.

Oh, and in case you're wondering: no, there's no seatbelt. The theory, apparently, is that in the event of a crash it's safer to be thrown a long way from the blades …

NISSAN

DELTAWING

IT MIGHT LOOK LIKE A STRANGE AMALGAM OF CONVERTIBLE RELIANT ROBIN AND SOMETHING FROM THE ANN SUMMERS STEALTH RANGE, but the Nissan Deltawing is nothing less than the most revolutionary race car of the twenty-first century. This is a racer that, with nothing more exotic than a 300bhp 1.6-litre turbo engine driving the rear wheels, can get round a track as quickly as a 600bhp V8 Indycar, burning just half the fuel while doing so. Even more impressive, it'll do so without tipping over.

'It looks completely counter-intuitive,' grins Ben Bowlby, the British designer of the Deltawing. 'It challenges your knowledge of what a race car is.' In 2008, sick of poring over IndyCar's rulebook to figure out which gaps in the regulations might yield a few milliseconds per lap, Bowlby set to work on a racer with IndyCar pace but half the power. He quickly realized this would require a car half the weight

of a conventional racer, one generating half the drag.

This explains the Deltawing's 'arrowhead' shape, which generates far less resistance than a race car with wide-spaced front tyres. Though it might look like a three-wheeler, there are actually two tyres up front, each only four inches wide.

So why doesn't it fall over, like Jeremy's Reliant? Well, the reason a Robin is topply is because all its weight sits over the narrow front end. In the Deltawing, the mass is all at the back, making it fantastically stable and, counter-intuitively, with more than enough grip at the front.

The Deltawing raced at the 2012 Le Mans 24 Hours (in its own 'experimental' category), demonstrating extraordinary pace before being cruelly punted out of the race by a Toyota. Still, Nissan had seen enough to believe the concept works: the Japanese company says it'll bring the Deltawing's layout and technology to an all-electric road car one day …

TOYOTA

GT86